To Patrick & Danielle, All ...

MW00613903

PARIS
201

Uncommon Places in the City of Light

A Bientôt A Paris!

Jerry Marterer

[signature]

Lydia Inglett Ltd. Publishing
Award-winning publishers of elegant books

Paris 201

Uncommon Places in the City of Light

ISBN: 978-1-938417-22-1

© 2015 Copyright Jerry Marterer

To order additional books, join our community and leave your comments: www.paris201.com

Published by Lydia Inglett Ltd. Publishing
www.lydiainglett.com
www.starbooks.biz
301 Central Ave. #181   Hilton Head Island, SC 29926
info@starbooks.biz

All rights reserved. No portion of this book may be reproduced, stored in a retrieval system, or transmitted in any form, or by any means—mechanical, electronic, photocopying, recording, or otherwise—without prior written permission from the publisher, except as provided by United States of America copyright law. Printed in China.

To order more copies of this or any of
our books, visit our on-line bookstore

www.STARBOOKS.biz

The place for beautiful, thoughtful gift books

The author and publisher make no claim to copyright of any material not original to the author's manuscript. This is a work of informational conveyance and as such, draws on research and sources at the time of writing. The publisher assumes no responsibility for furnished source materials. Every attempt to credit sources has been made. Although the author has made every effort to ensure that the information in this book is correct at press time, the author and publisher do not assume and hereby disclaim any liability to any party for any loss, damage, or disruption caused by errors or omissions, whether such errors or omissions result from negligence, accident, or any other cause.

*To my wife, Suzanne, for helping me
live my dream.*

"J'ai deux amours, mon pays et Paris"
"I have two loves, my country and Paris"

-JOSEPHINE BAKER,1931

TABLE OF CONTENTS

Lafayette and Washington

Thomas Jefferson

CHAPTER 1

Americans in Paris

Americans have been drawn to Paris since their nation was young. Part of the early attraction was the deep affection for General Lafayette, the French marquis who fought alongside General Washington to win our independence from England. Our near simultaneous revolutions that declared the rights of man created an affinity that continues to this day. In his book, *The Greater Journey*, David McCullough highlights the early attractions of medicine and art. In the early eighteen hundreds, the U.S. had few hospitals and no medical schools. Paris had large-scale hospitals, where teaching physicians would make daily rounds with medical students, including many Americans. Napoléon had just filled the Louvre with art liberated from his conquests. Its galleries, previously restricted to royalty, were opened to the public, with Sundays reserved for visiting foreigners.

Many Americans who arrived with the intention of staying a year or two never left. The French were just as fascinated with tales of the American frontier by authors such as James Fenimore Cooper and visits by Native American Indian chiefs. The Paris of today honors their American heroes with avenues Wilson, Roosevelt, Eisenhower, and Kennedy. A statue of General Washington standing alongside Lafayette looks over the P*lace des Etats-Unis* (United States Square). Thomas Jefferson's statue stands near the National Assembly where, as U.S. Minister to France, he worked with Lafayette on drafting France's *Declaration of the Rights of Man*.

Benjamin Franklin arrived in Paris in 1776 as an unofficial diplomat from a country that barely existed. His goal was to win support for America's war of independence. He was preceded by his reputation as a scientist and inventor and was warmly received by royalty and intellectuals. He eventually charmed the monarchy into providing the Americans military and financial aid. Ironically, the American ideals helped to inspire the French Revolution in 1789. Franklin lived in the village of Passy, now within the city limits. A

statue of the great American sits in a small garden called the square de Yorktown, which commemorates the battle of Yorktown, where a combined French and American army defeated the British in 1781. The mutual fascination between Parisians and Americans continues to this day with posters on kiosks in Paris advertising concert performances of American jazz

Ben Franklin in Passy

performers and gospel choirs, while Woody Allen draws crowds to his comedies about Americans in Paris.

Hemingway called Paris a moveable feast. The way I see it, each visitor carries home his or her own personal, private Paris: perhaps the taste of onion soup on a cold winter's day, the shabby chic of the one star hotel on that student trip, or the boulevard St-Germain on a rainy April evening. My first impression of Paris came on a business trip when I was in my 30s, not at all romantic or literary, but still vivid. On an industrial edge of the city, I went to lunch with some customers who used our packaging in their factory. A plain dining room served the surrounding facilities. After we were seated and shared a carafe of red wine at a table covered with brown paper, a large zucchini

American Gospel Choir

and tomato tart was brought to the table along with a basket of crusty bread. It was like nothing I had ever tasted. I must have shown my enthusiasm in eating it because I was quickly given a second helping, which I consumed with equal gusto. I was just about to say, "That was the best lunch I ever had," when a family size pot of boeuf bourgnignon was set in the middle of the table, followed by Camembert, crème brûlée, and coffee. I've had many culture shocks around the world since then, but none so pleasant. Over the next twenty years, I travelled regularly to Europe for business. Whenever possible, I would end the trips with a few days in Paris. In 2002 my son, who was working in Europe for a Dutch bank, mentioned that he wanted to buy a *pied*-à-*terre* (literally, a foot on the ground) in Paris. He asked me to help him look around on weekends when I was in Europe.

THE HUNT

Armed with the real estate section of *Le Figaro* we would pound the pavement around neighborhoods looking for open houses. It quickly became apparent that location, as in American cities, was everything. A studio apartment in the Marais district looked great in the afternoon, but a midnight recon showed that several quiet cafes turned into noisy S&M bars after dark. Another place in a Bohemian quarter was fine except for us having to step over a drunk sleeping in the building's doorway. Somewhat discouraged, we sat over coffee one morning and reviewed options. I had an idea. I proposed that instead of looking for a small studio, we should go together as partners and buy a larger place the family could use. I planned to retire sometime in the next

For Sale 3 room apartment

five to ten years, and the thought of living part time in Paris was sounding more and more attractive. He agreed enthusiastically, and we renewed our efforts.

THE DECISION TREE

Based on our previous experiences, I told him the best criteria for a neighborhood would be to eliminate any that his mother would not want to live in. That immediately narrowed our focus. The revised scope prompted us to use a decision tree approach. We made a list of the trade-offs and features:

• Low floor/high floor, elevator/no elevator. I had no desire to climb five flights of stairs in a nonelevator building, but living on the second floor meant no sunlight. We settled on elevator/high floor.

• A narrow street with less traffic, or a wide street to allow more light.

• *Gardienne* or no *gardienne*. Formerly known as a concierge, a *gardienne*, who lives on the ground floor, keeps the stairs and hallways clean, accepts deliveries, holds mail in the owner's absence, and, in some cases, for a modest hourly rate, will keep the apartment clean. Easy decision: *gardienne*.

• A newer building with modern heating and plumbing, or an older building with higher ceilings, older plumbing and character. Character won.

Paris 101 Menu

• Move-in condition or *travaux* à *prévoir* (Work required before move in).

• One bedroom with a living room sofa bed, or two bedrooms?

• Proximity to métro station, bus stop, taxi stand.

• Fresh food markets nearby—usually on pedestrian-only streets where the locals shop every day.

• Walkability: near major cultural attractions, but not in a heavy tourist zone.

• Near neighborhood restaurants and cafés that don't have menus in six languages or pictures of the food in the window.

Naturally, these trade-offs affected price and how many square feet for the money. We zeroed in on a neighborhood right away—the area around rue Cler, a market street near the Eiffel Tower and the Invalides. This quiet, middle class quarter had everything we wanted.

We had already done some research on the ins and outs of buying real estate and living in France. As an employee of a Dutch bank, my son was a Europen Union resident, so he could live anywhere in the European Union. As a visitor to France, I could stay ninety days at a time without a visa. In the unlikely event I needed to stay longer, I could always take the Eurostar train to London and back to renew my visitor status. It is generally no more difficult for Americans to buy real estate in France than it is for the French, which is not to say that it's easy. There is no multi-listing per se. Each quarter has independent realtors who resemble boutiques with photos in their windows describing their listings, so the selection of a neighborhood is important. For those who don't speak enough French to get by, there are English-speaking consultants who will search out properties that meet the buyer's criteria and guide them through the process—all for a fee of course. Apartments for sale are advertised by neighborhood in the *Le Figaro* newspaper. The Friday and Saturday editions list weekend open houses. The paper's website allows searching by neighborhood, number of rooms, and selling price. From our many viewings it's obvious that Parisian realtors give no advice at all on how to stage a property for showing, so be prepared for a dose of reality. The photos on the web listing show unmade beds, dirty dishes, and worse. I guess it comes down to ceiling height, square meters, number of rooms, and nothing else.

THE FIND AND THE OFFER

Over the next few months, my son spent every weekend looking at places in the rue Cler neighborhood, emailing me details and photos. In early 2003, on a quick visit, we saw a listing in the *Le Figaro* that looked interesting. We went to the realtor's office and learned that the apartment was vacant. A widow who had had sold it earlier as a *viager*, recently passed away. A *viager* is like an annuity, where a buyer pays an

The two buildings are separated by a courtyard for sunlight.

upfront amount or "bouquet" to the elderly owner-occupant who continues to live there, then the buyer makes a fixed monthly payment until the occupant's death, whereupon the buyer takes possession. This is a common type of sale in France used by older property owners that incorporates some elements of what we know as a reverse mortgage, except the buyer and seller are each making a bet on how long the seller is going to live. We went to see it with the realtor, first walking through a courtyard, then into a 1920s era building. A tiny two-person elevator took us to the fifth floor. The realtor climbed the stairs. There were two units on each floor. The stairwells were clean and nicely carpeted. We held back our opinions as we walked through the two small bedrooms, living room, bath, and galley kitchen, which for some reason the French call a *cuisine américaine*. The place needed everything. The kitchen was empty of appliances and cabinets. All that remained were a few pipes and some wires. The bath had an old tub and a small round toilet with a tank on the wall above and a pull chain. The walls were covered with a chalky white substance that came off on our hands. The floors were old uneven herringbone oak. It looked pretty depressing except for the view of the golden dome of the Invalides from the living room. In short, we loved it! As corporate nomads, we had already relocated a dozen times, and we knew what cleaning, painting, and kitchen and bath remodeling could do to transform a home. Our strategy was to offer the asking price, which appeared reasonable—a no-brainer you say. However in France, the seller is allowed to refuse it. We decided that I would pay my half in cash, and my son would finance his half. We filled out a *Promesse de Vente*, not quite a sales contract, but once accepted, it granted a sixty day option to buy the prop-

The view of the dome of the Invalides from our apartment window.

erty, subject to certain conditions. The required 10 percent deposit was paid. It was February, 2003. An eight month mating dance ensued, which we were told was not unusual. We needed to prove who we were, where we were born, and, in order to buy Euros and make an international wire transfer, that we were not financing terrorist activities. We learned all about the Napoléonic Code (Code Napoléon) and how it would impact us. Napoléon wanted to break the grip of royalty on France. His new code outlawed *primogéniture,* or the right of the first born son to inherit the entire estate as well as the title, thus perpetuating a hereditary upper class. He did this by mandating "forced heirship", where the assets of the deceased are required be divided evenly among the spouse and all of the children. He even provided that illegitimate children got a half share. This has lead over time to abandoned farms in rural France with several hundred owners. In France, it would have been impossible for Leona Helmsley to have left her fortune to her dog. We consulted a special lawyer who helped us sort this out. Oddly enough, the state of Louisiana still uses the Napoléonic Code for civil transactions while the other forty-nine states use the Uniform Commercial Code. At various times during the sale process, either party had the option to back out—neither had so far.

A PROBLEM

Two months into it, I got a call from my son. The inspector we hired discovered that the owner had connected the water pipes from our unit to the floor above in order to install a shower in a small studio made from two maid's rooms, known as *chambres de bonnes*. Most of the older apartment buildings provided each unit with a small room for a maid on the top floor, usually the sixth (in France the ground floor is always zero). The rooms were big enough for a single bed and not much more. The maids, primarily young immigrants from the rural provinces, shared a communal toilet and sink. Today few in the middle class have live in maids, and most of the rooms are rented out to students or used for storage. Because of the use of our plumbing, the studio could not be legally separated from the apartment below. We could either cancel the sale and get our deposit back or negotiate to have the studio included. We offered 10 percent more than the original price, and the seller accepted. The studio has become a self-contained guest quarters for visitors. When all the tax stamps were obtained, certificates issued, and notaries paid, on October 15 we finally took ownership—on paper at least. It would be another month before we could take possession and visit our new home away from home.

MOVING IN—ALMOST

On our first trip, we laid out a plan that would allow us to at least begin sleeping there as soon as possible. A friend recommended a painter. The walls would first need to be sanded down, meaning weeks of plaster dust, followed by painting. Then we could buy beds and some living room furniture, and we could use the primitive but functional bathroom while planning the next steps. We sent the painter a photograph of our living room in the U.S. that was finished in an ochre shade using a technique called sponging. He knew exactly what we meant and duplicated it perfectly. He then asked us to let him know what color we wanted on the woodwork. On an overnight stop in Paris, I brought a sample chip of white paint from home. He refused to use it because it was "incompatible." (I'm a guy. I thought white was white!) He said to come back the next day. I was staying at a hotel. When I returned the next afternoon, he had taken a palette and painted ten shades of white on the wainscoting. He described their nuances in order: mustard, eggshell, cream, snow, lemon, and so on. It was too much responsibility for me. He was not just a house painter: despite not wearing a beret and a white smock, he was an *artiste*! All of his dabs looked the same to me, so I told him to pick his favorite and use it. He seemed happy and obliged. He also got our heating system going before the freezing weather took hold. A gas-fired boiler in the kitchen circulated hot water through small iron radiators in each room and also served as a hot water heater. The pipes were all run outside of the walls near the ceiling, indicating that the gas heat was not original equipment. There were fireplaces in the living room and bedrooms, but the hearths were blocked with metal doors. I found out why when we visited our basement storage area called a cave. We were unable to get into it during the viewing because of a padlock and the absence of the owner, but now it was ours. The handyman dispatched the padlock with a swing of his hammer and we were in. The cave was stacked floor to ceiling with what appeared to be oval bricks of coal called *boulets*. "Ah yes", he said, "from the war." He told us it has long been illegal to burn it in fireplaces, which explained the retrofitted gas boiler. Wanting to rid ourselves of this wartime hoard, I asked if we could put it in the trash. No, that was illegal too. I went to the realtor's office and told him about our find. His reaction was the same. Since he spoke English, I told him that I was sure that in every city there were people who would do anything for a buck (in this case a Euro). Could he find some of those people and have them get rid of the coal? Four weeks and several hundred Euros later, *les boulets* had disappeared.

We were ready for the next projects, a new kitchen and bath. We selected a neighborhood contractor who made artistic drawings of what they would look like. We picked Italian cabinets and German appliances. Europeans understand small apartments. We settled on an 18-inch wide dishwasher and a high tech combination microwave/grill/oven, which we are still trying to learn to operate. The contract called for 45 percent upon signing, 50 percent upon delivery of equipment, and 5

Our new kitchen overlooking the courtyard

percent upon satisfactory completion. I explained that in the U.S. it was normal to hold back 10 percent as a better incentive for completion. The contractor explained that in France it's only 5 percent, because the customer always finds a reason not to pay it. I held my ground and they agreed on 10 percent. Maybe I gave up a 5 percent discount! Our building dates back to the 1920s, and it always seems to hold surprises after projects are started. First, it was the lack of an electrical ground, then the discovery of paper-wrapped wiring that was outlawed years ago and needed to be replaced. They became "add-ons" to the project cost. We told the contractor that we would be back in May, giving them more than the four months needed. He emailed photos at each stage of completion and used Google Translation to explain delays. I don't recommend using this software for any communication where details are important. One email explained in English that "The plumber is in the abyss." (?) For a laugh, try using Google to translate a paragraph from English into French. Then use it to translate the French back into English. It will have no resemblance to the original. In April, I received an email from the contractor asking which week in May we would arrive. Two weeks later the question was which day of the week would it be, and finally a few days before we left for Paris, what time of day would we arrive? I expected wet paint, but I now think the purpose of the last question was to time the delivery of the large bouquet of flowers in our living room when we arrived. I have learned two rules for projects in Paris:

They will not be completed on time or on budget.

They *will* be completed with precision and beautiful workmanship.

Original buildings on rue Cler

DISCOVERING THE NEIGHBORHOOD

Around the corner from our new home is the pedestrian-only rue Cler, the heart and soul of the quarter. This market street began showing up on maps of the city in the mid-eighteen hundreds. Two smaller buildings on the second block give an impression of how the neighborhood must have once looked. The legend is that Julia Child shopped here when she lived on the rue de l'Université. The shops specialize in flowers, fruits and vegetables, fish, meat, cheese, ice cream, chocolate, bread, and pastry. One shop still has a sign of a horse butcher but is now a crêperie. At the news stand we discovered *Pariscope*, a small magazine published each Wednesday that costs fifty cents. It lists all concerts, operas, plays, movies, and museum exhibits in Paris. Occasionally, we buy a

Former horse butcher on rue Cler

School day on rue Cler

The organ grinder is a fixture on rue Cler each Sunday morning.

Café du Marché

Sunday Morning on rue Cler

rotisserie chicken from *la boucherie* for dinner. The butcher always hands us a small jar of drippings because he assumes rightly that we

Rue Cler Rôtisserie Chicken sign

will make chicken soup the next day. We can stop next door and buy one leek, one carrot, and one stalk of celery instead of a plastic bag of ten, and a hand-tied *bouquet garni* from Provence for *la soupe*. On Saturday and Sunday the rue Cler is abuzz with locals. There is often an organ grinder or brass band entertaining on the corner. Three-generation-families gather for coffee or lunch at the Café du Marché, which is open every day, morning, noon, and night. This is not a café of intellectuals and existentialists like Les Deux Maggots or Café de Flore. This is where the local families come to enjoy each other's company. On Sunday the shops close around midafternoon and reopen on Tuesday morning.

The daily routine on rue Cler helped me to understand and appreciate the middle class Parisian lifestyle. I used to wonder about the quality of life for families raising children in an "inner city" environment, but I've learned a lot from my vantage point at the Café du Marché. In the morning, parents walk their young children to school. Then the moms meet at the café to catch up on news and gossip, before taking home a baguette and dinner ingredients. At lunchtime, those who work in the area pack the café to enjoy one of the *plats du jour*. Office workers in Paris are given daily lunch tickets (as part of their employment) that can be redeemed at neighborhood restaurants displaying a special decal. This practice supports family owned places and keeps employees happy. At the end of the school day, at 4:30, the moms line up in front of the school to wait for their children. With few exceptions, all children in Paris walk to and from school. The school lunch menus are very French, healthy, and delicious. Vivian Walt of *Time* magazine discovered when she moved to Paris that school lunches included a hors

Lunch Checks Accepted Here Window Decals

d'oeuvre, salad, main course, cheese, and dessert. Compare this "inner city" lifestyle to one of riding a suburban school bus with a brown bag peanut butter and jelly sandwich or dining on hot dogs and pizza in the school cafeteria.

I grew up in the 1950s in a small Pittsburgh neighborhood. On the main street there were two drugstores with lunch counters, a butcher, baker, fruit market, shoemaker, and a hardware store. Everyone could walk to them as well as to school. When I returned for my 50th high school reunion, they had all disappeared. Sure, school consolidations and economic conditions played a part, but maybe going back to the '50s is what I like so much about Paris neighborhoods. I hope they stay as they are. I have this fear that one 24-hour Walgreen's would wipe out half the businesses in our Parisian quarter. A Super Wallmart would kill off the rest of them like peasants in the black plague.

DEALING WITH THE FRENCH

In France, no detail is too small to overlook or minimize. It seems that everyone is an *artiste* and *connoisseur* with an opinion and not hesitant to share it. With the major projects completed, we turned to decorating; I bought some prints at an auction and took them to the frame shop down the street. The shop was a husband and wife operation. Their work is excellent. Madame was on duty that day. I selected the matting and a simple black frame that would make the prints stand out under lighting in the hallway. She refused to frame them in black, saying it was too somber. As we were arguing, a woman who lives in our building came in the shop and sided with Madame. When I explained the color of our walls, she relented. I now make sure that Monsieur is on duty before taking art to be framed. He never argues with me.

Our next visit was in the winter. It was freezing and I had forgotten to bring a scarf from the U.S. We were walking in the boulevard St-Germain-des-Près neighborhood and I stopped at a clothing store. Before I could ask about colors, I saw the 400 Euro price tag and decided to shop in a less trendy neighborhood closer to home. The

Rue Cler Fruits et légumes

Rue Cler Charcuterie

Rue Cler Fromagerie

Cler Fleurs

prices there were reasonable. I asked the sales clerk if the scarf came in burgundy, a popular color at the time. The clerk replied, in French of course, "Not in burgundy, but we have it in Bordeaux." I checked to see if he was smiling at his joke but he was absolutely serious. Burgundy and Bordeaux are two of my favorite red wines and later I poured a glass of each and compared them. There may be a slight difference in color, but I still can't figure out how it would show on a scarf. To the French, the distinction was important.

At times, negotiations are in order. We are spoiled in the U.S. when we have our dry cleaning returned in a day or two. When I take our clothes to the cleaners on rue Cler, it's always the same. After paying in advance, I ask when I can have it back. If it's Monday, the answer is *lundi*. "But that's next week!" I protest. "How about Friday?" They reply, "*Alors, samedi*" (Saturday). I walk away feeling like I won a concession.

Some interactions end in a standoff. The French word is *bras de fer*, or arm wrestling. I use my French debit card to get Euros from my French bank account at the ATM in my neighborhood. One Friday evening, the ATM rejected my card. Other ATM's did as well, despite the fact that my account held plenty of cash. I had to wait until Monday to confront my banker. He said that I was only permitted to withdraw a set amount of Euros per week, and I had exceeded it. An argument ensued where the only French I could muster was, "But it's MY money!" His arguments were more complex and emphatic; essentially, the bank was protecting me from myself. I had run out of verbal ammunition after the first salvo. How come French language courses never teach you how to argue in French? When the banker was certain he had won, he allowed me to make a withdrawal on a one time basis.

POLITESSE

There is a saying in the U.S.: "Little things mean a lot." In fact, I think it was even the name of a song in the 1950s. In France, however, little things mean EVERYTHING! One of the first important lessons we learned was that understanding French does not mean that you understand the French. They fought a bloody revolution to gain their status as equals, free of the rigid hierarchy of royalty. After 1789, they addressed each other as "citizen" to reflect this newfound status, later evolving to Monsieur and Madame. The politeness or *politesse* that characterizes day-to-day interactions in France has its roots in the revolution, but it's not just a matter of being polite. It has more to do with respect when the butcher, bus driver, or store clerk expects to be greeted with "*Bonjour Monsieur*" or "*Bonjour Madame*" (or "*Bonsoir*" after 6:00 pm). Failure to do so is considered not merely impolite but downright disrespectful. The same code applies on leaving. An "*Au revoir Monsieur (or Madame)*" is mandatory. When I hear from returning American vacationers that the French are rude, I ask them to describe the situation. More often than not, there was a violation of the code of *politesse* which actually meant the American was being rude, albeit unknowingly. A wonderful book on why the French do what they do is *French or Foe*, by Polly Platt. It should be required reading for Paris 201. She tells readers to learn several "magic words" in French that will endear them to the natives and keep them out of trouble. Five of the words are the phrase in French: "*Excusez-moi de vous déranger*" (Excuse me for disturbing you), which never fails to elicit someone's help. Others, such as please (*s'il vous plaît*) and thank you (*merci*), followed by *Monsieur* or *Madame*, are not unlike what we were taught as children but have forgotten to use as we grew older. Spoken French has its own cadence, timbre, and body language. By observing and listening, it's possible to learn what I call "situational French", how real people order in cafés, how they greet each other and carry on conversations. This varies with age group with more slang from youth and more formality among adults. It often bears little resemblance to what is learned from textbooks. Paris is a big busy city and even the French who live in the provinces will tell you that Parisians can be brusque in their own way, not unlike Midwesterners describing New Yorkers. Recently, the City of Paris has begun taking Parisians to task for violating their own code of *politesse*. Perhaps the stress of the poor economy and high unemployment is taking its toll.

A sign in buses reminds riders that "*2 bonjours font 1 bon jour*" (Two bonjours make for one good day). In the métro, large posters

2 Bonjours...

decry pushing and shoving while boarding the métro.

PARIS 201

Our time in Paris was still limited to weekends tacked onto business trips and short vacations each year, sometimes with children and grandchildren in tow. We roamed flea markets and neighborhood antique fairs to complete the decorating and furnishing. When I retired six years later, our stays in Paris became measured in months and touched all of the seasons. Spring featured new vegetables, white asparagus, and lamb. Summer brought raspberries, strawberries, and cantaloupe from Provence. In the fall, it was partridge, venison, hare, wild boar, thick sauces with chestnuts, and a dozen varieties of mushrooms and oysters. Winter brought rain and a few snow flurries. Our lives there changed from jet-lagged tourists eager to do "Paris 101", to residents ready to live like Parisians, (without the hassle of having to work there). We began to see things around us that we had overlooked earlier during our hurried visits. Instead of rushing to try new restaurants every day, we started shopping on the rue Cler and cooking at home. We roamed the city with no particular agenda or schedule, and we learned to use métros and buses instead of taxis. We studied daily life, got to know neighbors and shopkeepers, and visited museums unknown to most tourists. Seemingly unrelated places suddenly

Rue Cler Raspberries

Fall Mushrooms

Oysters on rue Cler

appeared connected by common threads. It is said that a stranger in a strange land has the keenest eye. As we discovered new layers of culture and history, stereotypes melted away and Paris began making sense. It became a self-study course we call *Paris 201*.

"Paris 101" is important and should not be taken lightly. Hitting the high points should be your goal on the first visit. Riding the red,

Paris 101 Big Bus

open top bus past the Eiffel Tower, Arc de Triomphe, Notre-Dame, the Louvre, and other landmarks in the two-hour circle tour is a great way to start out, particularly if you only have few days in the city. One and two day passes include unlimited stops. Wait in line for a ride to the top of the Eiffel Tower. Ride the tour boats up and down the Seine. Have a picnic in one of the parks with a baguette sandwich and a bottle of wine. Linger in a café while reading *Pariscope*. You may walk around with a map in your hand,

but each day in Paris will move you further along the learning curve. Despite what you may hear, Parisians really do like Americans and will help with directions and shopping or restaurant rec-

Paris 101 Tour Boat

ommendations. It seems they have all either visited or plan to visit the U.S. They love our music and watch our television shows, but I sometimes wish that dubbed versions of the *Simpsons* and *Jerry Springer* were not so dominant in representing our culture.

Paris 201 doesn't dwell on things that aren't there anymore, except to explain something real that exists today. Long gone restaurants, hotels, and buildings are consigned to history. The Paris of today contains enough vintage authenticity in its neighborhoods that nothing needs to be left to the imagination except the faces and voices of the original inhabitants.

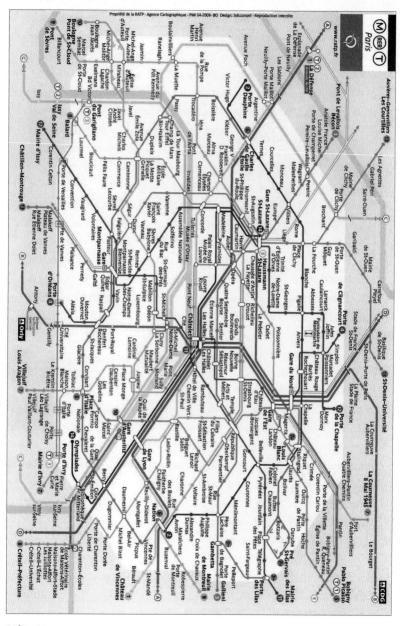

Métro Map

CHAPTER 2

Métros, Buses, Trains and Boats

T he first métro in Paris opened in 1900, not so much to benefit commuters, but for the Universal Exhibition of the same year. The aptly named No 1 Métro travelled across the city, between two former gates, the porte Maillot in the west, and the porte de Vincennes in the east. The original stops were designed around the exhibits along the Champs-Elysées. Motorized buses didn't appear until 1905. Today, there are fourteen métro lines and over sixty bus routes that stop within a few blocks of any destination. Each métro line starts near one end of the city's oval shape, winds through town, and terminates near another end. The *Plan du métro de Paris* looks like a mess of tangled string. Often, you will need to make a "*correspondance*" and change trains at an intersection where métro lines cross. Some of these major crossings, like Concorde, are infamous for rush hour madness and, at the same time, famous for their good musicians. There are also the Regional Express (RER) trains that extend the reach of the métro system out to the suburbs.

Correspondance

The Paris métro and bus system should be viewed as an ensemble that gives a visitor ultimate flexibility. Métro tickets can be used on buses, however a ticket purchased on a bus cannot be used on the métro. A métro ticket can only be used once. Keep it handy because the métro agents may ask to see it at the exit. A bus ticket is good for the next ninety minutes on any other bus.

In 2015, métro and bus tickets cost 1.80 Euros. A *carnet* of ten costs 14.40 Euros. The real bargain is the *Paris Visit* Pass that is good for UNLIMITED travel on buses and métros. The most popular are the three day pass for 26.50 Euros and the five day pass for 38.20 Euros. A

Buying Tickets

slightly cheaper and more flexible option is to buy several one day passes for 7.00 Euros, especially if you will have days without using a bus or métro. All of these are sold at any métro station using a credit card or cash machine. For a little more, the ticket can include the suburban trains (RER) for excursions. Caution! Métro and bus tickets have a magnetic strip down the center. Storing them close to your cell phone or a magnetic clasp on a purse will demagnetize them and they will not work. We learned this the hard way, but the attendant at the métro station tested and (cheerfully!) replaced them.

THE BUS VERSUS THE MÉTRO

Most visitors to Paris figure out the métro system but don't consider using the bus system because the routes are less visible. However, the bus has several advantages over the métro:

1) If you need to change métro lines to reach your destination, there is a good chance that a bus will go there directly. In other words, the systems are designed to complement each other.

2) There are four times as many bus lines as métro lines. In our neighborhood we have only one métro but six bus lines to choose from.

Paris Bus

3) There are no stairs to descend or climb. The bus actually lowers itself to the curb when it stops.

4) Buses can avoid the worst traffic since the main streets have bus-only lanes.

5) Buses offer free sightseeing as you cross the city. Some buses are legendary like the No 69 which drives right through the courtyard of the Louvre past the I. M. Pei glass pyramid.

6) There are never any vagrants sleeping on a bus and no entertainers expecting money.

7) For some reason, bus riders are more genial. The driver greets everyone, and younger riders will usually stand so that older folks can sit.

8) Riding a bus across Paris is a nice rainy day activity.

Métros, on the other hand:
1) Move more people at one time.

2) Run more frequently.

3) From point to point, métros beat buses for speed, since there is no traffic to slow them.

4) They start earlier in the morning and run later at night.

5) All métros run every day but some bus routes do not operate on Sundays or holidays.

6) The métro passes through hundreds of obscure stations under neighborhoods that many riders, even Parisians, never get to see. This intrigues me. Above the ground there are places called Oberkampf, Bir-Hakeim, Victor Hugo, and La Muette, a veritable pantheon of landmarks, heroes, and military victories.

No 10 Métro

Armed with a métro/bus pass, I set out to go where no tourist has ever gone. It may take years to do them all, but here is one of my first expeditions.

THE NUMBER 8 MÉTRO

One of the reasons for being on my list of favorites is that it's the only one that runs through my neighborhood. No matter my destination, I begin with the No 8. Like all the other métros, it begins its run at 5:30 am. We feel the faint, gentle rumbling below as we are waking up, assuring us that we are still in the city of our dreams. Over the years I have discovered that its arc shaped route through central Paris

holds surprises at almost every station, some famous, some mysterious, and some gems of history that are hidden in plain sight. There is the ease and simplicity of not having to change métro lines, never wandering too far from the station, and, at least for me, taking the same

No 8 Métro

train all the way back home at the end of the day. Besides, it's hard to feel like a tourist as long as the lavender number 8 circle is in sight. Even if you are on your way somewhere else and find yourself at one of these stops, it's worth it to go up and learn something.

AROUND THE ECOLE MILITAIRE

The Ecole Militaire Métro stop is at the corner of avenue Bosquet and avenue de la Motte-Picquet in the 7th Arrondissement on the left bank. It's only a block from our apartment. It is also in the middle of a great neighborhood to set up your Paris headquarters since it has good affordable two and three star hotels, small family owned restaurants with daily menus on a chalk board, a pedestrian-only market street where the locals shop, and within a block, three of the most iconic Paris sights.

Straight ahead is the Ecole Militaire, built by King Louis XV in 1760 as one of the pet projects of his official mistress, Madame de Pompadour. (Whatever happened to the title of official mistress?) Its original mission was to train and commission the sons of fallen

Ecole Militaire

French army officers and children from poor families. Its most famous alumnus was Napoléon Bonaparte. The two divisions, cavalry and artillery, have their own schools on the left and right of the main hall. The church can be entered via the door in the center. It displays the battle flags that honor the school's distinguished graduates. Although it now houses military offices, the army's equestrian team still practices their moves in the field behind the Ecole Militaire.

In front of the school is its former parade ground, the Champs de Mars (the field of Mars, the god of war), which was used for the Universal Exposition of 1889, where pavilions from around the world showcased their countries' arts, crafts, and technology. The only remaining exhibit, the Eiffel Tower, stands at the opposite end of the Champs de Mars. It was the tallest man-made structure in the world until New York's Chrysler Building was finished in 1930. Visitors can walk up the stairs to the first level, which holds an ice skating rink in the winter months, or take the elevator to the second level or to the very top. The second level has a good quality family cafe, and the top level holds the Jules Verne, a Michelin starred restaurant that has a six month waiting list for a reservation and requires a high credit card

Champs de Mars and Eiffel Tower

Peace Memorial

limit. There is a children's carousel at the foot of the tower. The tower was only supposed to stay up until its builders were compensated for the cost via admission fees over the next twenty years, and many leading Parisians were looking forward to being rid of the monstrosity. However, Marconi's invention of the wireless telegraph in 1907 gave Paris, overnight, the world's highest radio antenna and it was saved.

After dark, on the hour, 20,000 strobe lights dazzle for ten minutes. A more recent addition is the Wall for Peace, placed ironically in front of the Ecole Militaire on the Champs de Mars. The word peace is written on glass panels in thirty-two languages. It was built for the city's millennium celebration, and was only supposed to stand for four months. While the spirit of the memorial is universally accepted, the design is not. My son says it looks like something bought at IKEA and assembled badly.

Eiffel Tower at Night

Hôtel des Invalides

Two blocks east of the Ecole Militaire Métro stop stands the massive complex of the Hôtel des Invalides, built by King Louis XIV as a hospital and retirement home for aged and invalid soldiers. It was constructed in 1679 in a field outside city walls. The domed royal chapel was added in 1708. Today, it houses military offices and an impressive army museum. Many war heroes are interred here, most notably Napoléon Bonaparte, whose remains were brought from St Helena in 1840. His tomb and the Eiffel Tower are usually on everyone's "Paris 101" list. The gold dome, majestically illuminated at night, was regilded in 1989 using a half a million dollars worth of gold leaf.

And now back to the Ecole Militaire Métro stop. Every métro line runs in both directions. The station at

Le Dôme at Night

the last stop becomes the direction. The No 8 travels between Balard and Créteil. The stops we will visit are in the direction of Créteil. On the return, the direction will be Balard. Make your choice before descending to the platform. You will need at least a one day métro pass.

Métro Direction

CONCORDE

Once the métro starts moving from the Ecole Militaire it will pass the stops of La Tour-Maubourg and Invalides, then go under the River Seine and back up to the Concorde stop on the right bank. This stop serves Métro lines 1, 8, and 12, so during rush hours it's a bit frenetic. If you are changing lines, which we are not today, you may have a bit of a walk. Fortunately the acoustics are great for the underground musical performers. My personal favorites are the Russian choir and the chamber orchestra. They are all good enough that I usually drop some change in their baskets. They also sell CDs of their music. Performers are granted permits to play in métro stations by the transit authority based on auditions held each year. There are also unlicensed itinerants who board the métro cars and recite poetry or sing. Unless you wish to donate, it's best to avoid eye contact, foot tapping, or singing along. Otherwise you will incur their wrath for enjoying but not paying.

Métro Concorde

At the Concorde stop take the exit for the rue Royale. You will see a busy eight sided square built by Louis XV and originally named for him. It is also a major traffic intersection and the first non-enclosed square built in Paris. There is a Ferris wheel operating there during the winter. The square originally held a statue of Louis XV in the center. It was destroyed during the revolution and temporarily replaced by a guillotine that operated on a daily basis to the roar of crowds. Its most famous victims were King Louis XVI and Marie Antoinette in 1793. It

Hôtel Crillon and the Ministry of the Navy

was called the Place de la Révolution for a few years and later renamed the Place de la Concorde as a way of putting the bad days behind it. In 1833, a 3000-year-old obelisk, donated by the Viceroy of Egypt, was placed in the spot where the guillotine had stood. The obelisk is the oldest monument in Paris, although many Parisians would not be able to answer the trivia question. The two fountains were added at around the same time. Around the octagon are statues honoring the then eight major cities, other than Paris, of France.

The 360 degree panorama around the Place de la Concorde shows off some of the finest glories of Paris. To the west is the beginning of the Champs-Elysées with the Arc de Triomphe visible at the other end.

In December a Christmas market operates at the start of the Champs-Elysées, which is lighted for the season. On the north side where you exited the métro are twin classical buildings constructed by Louis XV, the Hôtel Crillon on the left and

Champs Elysées at Christmas

Arc de Triomphe, the Western view from the Concorde

View of National Assembly from rue Royale

the Ministry of the Navy on the right. Between the twin buildings is the rue Royale which ends at the columned Church of the Madeleine (our next stop). Across the Seine in the opposite direction is a similar columned facade. This is the Palais Bourbon built for the daughter of Louis XIV. It has become the seat of the National Assembly. The Roman portico was added by Napoléon as an esthetic to make a mirror image of the Madeleine. Looking east you will see the beginning of the Tuileries Gardens and the former site of another palace.

Les jardins des Tuileries

The Tuileries Palace once connected the now open ends of the Louvre. It was built by Catherine de Medici, widow of Henri II in the late 1500s. Before he built Versailles, Louis XIV resided there. The name comes from the old clay pits on the banks of the Seine where roof tiles (tuiles) had been produced. Louis XVI was moved there

Nicolas Raguenet, *Tuileries Palace*, Musée Carnavalet

from Versailles and kept under house arrest until he and his wife were beheaded. Napoléon made it his imperial residence and it was used during the restoration by King Louis Philippe. Napoléon III (Bonaparte's nephew) lived there until he was deposed and sought exile in England. The Tuileries Palace was destroyed by an angry mob during an uprising in 1871, along with the historic city hall. The end buildings of the Louvre were saved and restored. Ironically, nearly all of the damage ever done to Paris has been done by the Parisians themselves. Today, the space between Concorde and the Louvre is made up of beautiful gardens. Two long outbuildings remain at the edge of the Place de la Concorde and one is an absolute must see. On the left is the former

Jeu de Paume

Musée de l'Orangerie

royal tennis court building, the Jeu de Paume, which now hosts photography exhibits. On the right is the Orangerie where fruit was once grown for the royalty in the winter months. It is now a magnificent art museum.

In 1927, Claude Monet donated a series of large oil paintings showing seasonal scenes of water lilies to the City of Paris who installed them as wraparound murals in two rotundas in the Orangerie. These rooms have been called the Sistine Chapel of Impressionism. Then in the 1960s a large collection of Impressionist and postimpressionist paintings was donated to the museum. This wonderful collection is covered in chapter 4 in more detail.

MADELEINE

The next stop is Madeleine, but you can easily walk up the rue Royale to reach it instead of using the métro. The Place de la Madeleine is a compact square filled by the imposing church dedicated to

Saint Mary Magdalene. If it looks more like a Roman temple, there is a reason. Louis XV decided to build a church here to honor this early saint. It never got beyond the foundation phase and changed architects

Eglise de la Madeleine from Concorde

several times before the events of the revolution put a halt to construction. Napoléon decided to make it a temple to honor the military, but after his fall it was finally completed and consecrated as a church to the

original honoree, Mary Magdalene. It is said to be the only church in Paris without a window. The church is also a venue for evening performances of sacred music by Handel, Mozart, and Vivaldi. If you stand on the front steps and look straight out you will see the mirror image of the

La Madeleine Interior

Baccarat

Place Madeleine Flower Market

portico across the Seine at the National Assembly. A counter clockwise walk around the church will start at the old flower market which appears in many works of art. Further down is Fauchon, the fashionable food emporium. Behind the church is the Pinacothèque de Paris, a new, privately funded art museum. Make a mental note to come back and visit it after reading about it in chapter 6. Around the next corner of the square sits Fauchon's competitor, Hédiard and several foie gras and caviar shops. Both Fauchon and Hédiard have good, if a bit pricey, restaurants for lunch. The Baccarat crystal store occupies the corner of the boulevard Malesherbes. This is definitely an up market métro stop. To the west down the boulevard sits the church of St-Augustin, built during the Haussmann era under Napoléon III to decorate a sharply angled intersection. The Byzantine structure was built around one of the first cast iron frames .

Pinacothèque Museum Poster

Caviar Kaspia

St-Augustin view from
Place de la Madeleine

Opéra Garnier

OPÉRA

The next métro stop is Opéra, which is at the crossroads of the No 8, 3, and 7 lines. Emerging from the Place de l'Opéra exit you will be struck by the sight of a Second Empire baroque palace topped by two gilded statues and rose marble columns. Napoléon III's reconstruction of Paris led to a new square around a new opéra house, designed by Charles Garnier, with the largest footprint of any opéra house in the world. An underground lake delayed completion until 1875. The small lake still exists and was featured in *The Phantom of the Opéra*.

The interior is even more exquisite with crystal chandeliers, elaborate foyers, plenty of velvet, and a more recent ceiling mural by Chagall. Daily tours are offered. In 1989, a new opéra house was built in the Place de la Bastille to make performances more accessible to

Chagall Mural, Opéra Garnier

the masses. The new (and ugly, in my opinion) Opéra Bastille now hosts the classical operas and the Opéra Garnier specializes in dance.

On the left of the square is the Café de la Paix, where post performance audiences have stopped for late dinners for over a century. Looking down the rue de la Paix you will see the column in the Place Vendôme that was erected by Napoléon to celebrate his victory at Austerlitz. Behind the Opéra are the

Café de la Paix

two best reasons for bringing your credit card on this tour: Galeries Lafayette and Printemps, Paris's most famous department stores.

Place Vendôme view from Place de l'Opéra

Printemps has an elegant restaurant under a stained glass dome. If you happen to be there in December, be sure to take in the legendary animated musical store windows. Each year the two stores seem to compete for the most over-the-top themes.

Restaurant under the dôme in Printemps

Printemps

RICHELIEU-DROUOT

Our next four stops will uncover sights and experiences that most tourists never see. It is *La Vie Parisienne*. They are all in older neighborhoods and may be taken for granted by the locals, but each is a unique slice of city life. One stop over from the Opéra is Richelieu-Drouot. This stop is served by both the No 8 and No 9 lines. Exit for the rue Drouot and follow it for a block. The neighborhood is known for the Hôtel Drouot, the oldest auction house in Paris, going back to 1852, where up to sixteen auctions may be happening at the same time.

Hôtel Drouot

The 1980s era building that replaced the original is not inspiring, but what goes on inside is exciting. Every day, it opens at 11:00 am. You can browse all the auction rooms that feature everything from masterpieces to shabby chic in fine art, furniture, vintage clothing and handbags, books, china, and rugs. Viewing is both the day before and the morning of each auction, but at noon sharp it closes for lunch and everyone heads to the bistros that fill the quarter. At 1:00 pm the doors reopen and the hammers start falling at 2:00 pm. It's not necessary to preregister to bid, but you need to know your French numbers. If you are the lucky high bidder, credit cards are accepted. Be advised that a

Drouot Auction Action

buyer's premium and value added tax (called TVA in French) can add up to 30 percent to the winning bid. Whether you are a bidder or not, just going from room to room and watching the action is worth a visit. Upcoming auctions can be previewed on line at Drouot.com.

GRANDS BOULEVARDS

The next stop will be Grands Boulevards. Walk back to the Richelieu-Drouot Métro and either hop on for a short ride or walk to the east along the boulevard Montmartre to the Musée Grévin, a wax museum built in 1882. Every Parisian was sure to visit as a child. It's an eclectic mix of history, nostalgia, and kitsch: Robespierre, Marat in his bathtub, Elton John, Mother Theresa, and Michael Jackson. Everyone should go at least once, but that is not why we came to this métro stop. To the left of the façade of the Musée Grévin is the entrance to the passage Jouffroy, an 1847

Musée Grévin

version of a shopping mall. At the time, Paris was not yet pedestrian friendly with horse drawn transportation, muddy streets, and a lot of unheated buildings. The first passages appeared in the late 1700s. There are still over a dozen remaining in Paris, and this neighborhood has some of the most quaint and lively ones. Jouffroy was the first heated passage, and today is populated by family owned specialty shops for expensive toys and games, gourmet candy, posters, and art books. It even has its own hotel, the Chopin.

Across the boulevard Montmartre is the Passage des Panoramas, built in 1800 with a similar glass roof and mosaic floor. It was the first passage to have gas lights. It is the narrowest and most original

Passage Verdeau

of the passages. Restaurants spill out into the passage, interspersed with dealers of stamps and vintage autographs. This is a prime neighborhood to explore these relics of another age since back through the passage Jouffroy and across the street is the passage Verdeau. Antique and art galleries, framing shops, and cafes are the

Passage Jouffroy Interior

Passage Jouffroy

"Passages were the first indoor shopping arcades. A dozen still remain in Paris."

Hôtel Chopin

Passage des Panoramas

Passage des Panoramas Interior

norm here. The passages are relatively unknown to tourists and with the Musée Grévin, they make up our favorite rainy day option when we have visitors, although we also stop here for lunch when we attend auctions at Drouot.

One of the city's most venerable dining spots, the Bouillon Chartier, is a few blocks away on the rue du Faubourg-Montmartre. It opened as a "bouillon" serving soup to hungry workers two centuries ago. A monument to Parisian life, it is cavernous, crowded, noisy, and inexpensive, with simple old style cooking. Brusque waiters will write your order on the paper table covering. The waiters are charged for what they bring from the kitchen and settle up at the end of their shifts,

Bouillon Chartier

providing the incentive for them to collect from the customers they serve. There are cabinets of small drawers throughout the place. These were for daily regulars to store their napkins which were washed once a week, a practice that was outlawed years ago as unsanitary, but the drawers remain in many old time restaurants.

STRASBOURG-ST-DENIS

From the Grands Boulevards stop, the Number 8 next passes through the Bonne Nouvelle station, named after the nearby Church

Métro Bonne Nouvelle

of Notre-Dame de Bonne-Nouvelle, (Our Lady of Good News). The only remarkable feature is the whimsical wavy station sign.

The next stop, Strasbourg-St-Denis is a hidden cache of Paris history. A street map that indicates the No 8 Métro stops shows that we are travelling under streets that form an arc beginning and ending at the River Seine. This arc traces one of the old city walls on the right bank built by Charles V, from 1356 to 1383. The word boulevard comes from bulwark, or defensive wall. As Paris expanded, whenever a wall was demolished and the surrounding moat filled in, an instant right of way was created that became a wide boulevard, in this case a series of boulevards. Early métro lines followed the wide boulevards for a reason. It was easier and cheaper to simply dig up

Wall of Charles V, at top of map

the street, build the tracks and walls, cover them with vaulted iron roofs, fill them over, and rebuild the streets. Exit for the rue St-Martin. A magnificent triumphal arch rises from the street and two blocks to the left, across the boulevard de Strasbourg, stands another one

Métro Construction

even more detailed. These arches straddle two ancient roads that lead out of Paris, the rue St-Denis and the rue St-Martin. Each was a *porte* (gate) in the wall that we are travelling under. Even after the walls of Charles V were torn down, the old roads into the city were still the

Vaulted roof in No 8 Metro

main access and the gates were used to collect tolls on goods entering Paris. Both the porte St-Denis arch, built in 1672, and the porte St-Martin in 1674 were erected by Louis XIV. They are both inscribed "Louis the Great" in Latin

(*Ludovico Magno*) and are covered with statuary and bas reliefs depicting military victories. The rue St-Denis follows the first road in Paris built by the Romans leading north. It became the route for royal processions entering Paris from the Cathedral of St-Denis, the first gothic church ever built and the burial place of kings and queens. The arches sit right in the middle of the street in a busy working class

Porte St-Denis

Porte St-Martin

neighborhood where absolutely no one appears to give them a second thought. The term "working class" takes on a new meaning, however, in the streets south of the arches, so it's best to head back to the métro.

RÉPUBLIQUE

Twelve streets and five métro lines converge on the Place de la République. A bastion on the wall of Charles V stood here when it was a city gate, known as the porte du Temple. Take the No 4 exit for the rue du Faubourg du Temple and look back at the square. It is dominated by a statue of a woman known as Marianne, representing the French Republic. Her image is based on the Delacroix painting, *Liberty leading the People*. The square is often the scene of demonstrations by the Parisian left. Walk away from the statue two blocks and turn left on the quai de Valmy.

Place de la République

This is the Canal St-Martin, which Napoléon ordered built in 1802. It connected the River Ourcq to the Seine, to supply fresh water, food, and building materials to a growing city. The wrought iron bridges over the canal will look familiar to fans of the movie, *Amélie*, where the title character, played by Audrey Tautou, is seen skipping stones across the water. The canal comes out of its underground passage here and heads north to the Rotonde de la Villette, one of the toll barriers that marked the city limits of Paris in the late 1700s. Its function was to collect taxes on goods entering the city. Today it houses a

Canal St-Martin Locks

restaurant. A modern bicycle path along the Canal d'Ourcq takes riders out of the city to quaint country villages. A walk from here to the

Rotonde de la Villette

La Marine

Bassin de Villette where the Ourcq meets the canal is a mile, but only four blocks up the canal are two good places for lunch, La Marine, at 55 bis quai de Valmy, and Le Verre Volé, at 67 rue de Lancry, where it meets the quai de Valmy. Immediately across the canal from there is the Hôtel du Nord. Its fame originates from the 1938 film of the same name, and its legacy continues. Live events open to the public in-clude theme nights and vintage jazz concerts. They have a following among young Parisians. To the right, the canal goes under the street and emerges in the Place de la Bastille in a marina known as the Arsenal. To continue the tour, return to the métro stop.

Hôtel du Nord

Cirque d'Hiver

FILLES DU CALVAIRE

The next stop, Filles du Calvaire, is named after a Benedictine order of nuns (Daughters of Calvary) which existed before the revolution. At the top of the stairs, in front of the métro exit, is the Cirque d'Hiver, or winter circus. The immense round ediface looks like a circus tent with Greek columns, which serve the intended purpose of supporting a big top without center poles. In the Musée d'Orsay, George Seurat's painting depicts a day here at the circus. This is a circus the way it used to be with lion tamers, acrobats, high wire-walkers, clowns, bareback riders, and circus acts from around the world, performing to the music of a full orchestra. The leotard was invented here by a trapeze artist of the same name. The handsome men and beautiful women of the Bouglione family

Georges Seurat, *Le Cirque*, Musée d'Orsay

have been performing in the show since 1930. The audience is of all ages. It is a national treasure to be taken in time and time again since the show changes every year. There are matinée and evening shows Friday through Sunday and a matinée on Wednesday afternoon, a no

school day in France. To the left of the building is the Clown Bar, a fixture for pre-show lunch or dinner featuring traditional bistro fare. The circus operates only in the winter months before going on the road in the summer, but between April and September the historic arena is used for staging operas and other spectacles in the round.

The Clown Bar

BASTILLE

We are now headed for the last stop on this tour, the Place de la Bastille. On the way we will pass the stops of St-Sébastien-Frossart, and Chemin Vert. At the bastille stop, exit for the Opéra Bastille to get an unobstructed view of the entire square. Just as our first stop on the right bank, the Place de la Concorde, marked the spot where France's absolute monarchy ended at the guillotine, the Place de la Bastille marks the beginning of that end. The bastille was a fortification next to the porte St-Antoine, the last gate of Charles V's wall that we have been following underground. Built as a defensive fortress in the 1400s, by the time of Louis XVI its eight towers came in handy for political prisoners, out of favor royalty and troublesome protestants. The area immediately inside the eastern walls included the fashionable Marais. Outside the walls however, was

the Faubourg-St-Antoine, a volatile working class neighborhood, where one can still find family owned furniture makers. There was also a paper factory and tapestry looms.

Much has been written about Louis XVI and the basis for the French Revolution. Paris was tense during the

Jean-Pierre Houël, *Prise de la Bastille,* **Bibliothèque National, Paris**

summer of 1789. The previous year's harvest was poor and the winter especially severe. Louis was disliked by some of the Paris nobility who fomented overthrow as well as by the bourgeoisie and the poor. The first riots occurred earlier in the spring in the Faubourg-St-Antoine as rumors of forced wage cuts at the paper factory swept the district. The factory was burned and looted. Troops arrived and shot many of the rioters, while the mill owner fled to the safety of the bastille. Then on July 14, the mob began looking for arms from city arsenals and, joined by mutinous soldiers, broke in to the Invalides, taking cannon and muskets. The bastille was a symbol of repression as well as the only fortress remaining in Paris at the time so that's where the mob went. The commander of the bastille surrendered it to the mob on the condition that he and his men would be spared. They were executed shorly after by the revolutionaries who put their heads on pikes. After the sacking of the fortress all of Paris seemed to join in the wanton spree of death and destruction that lasted for several years. Louis XVI and Marie Antoinette were executed in 1793 back at what is now the Place de la Concorde.

By the end of 1789, the bastille had been completely demolished. Today, the outlines of the fortress are marked by special paving

Outline of the Bastille

stones in the street. In 1793 a fountain was installed and it formally became the Place de la Bastille. Napoléon proposed a giant bronze elephant on the site. The project only got as far as a plaster copy that deteriorated and was eventually removed as an eyesore. The present July Column was inaugurated in 1840, although not to celebrate July 14, but to mark the three day July revolution of 1830 that deposed Charles X. It is topped by a bronze, torch-bearing winged statue called the Spirit of Liberty. The bastille and the neighborhoods of Eastern Paris continue to be at the center of demonstrations and strikes to this day.

July Column

To the south, there is a large marina that comes off the Seine known as the Arsenal. You may see a tour boat disappearing under the square. This is the beginning of the Canal St-Martin. Half of its route was paved over in the 1960s. It runs under the

Arsenal Marina

boulevard Richard Lenoir for about a mile, then opens up on a nice promenade. There is a canal boat tour from the Seine marina operated by Canauxrama.

The Opéra Bastille was built on the site of the old bastille rail station in 1989. If you walk down the street that goes along the right side of the building, the rue de Lyon, bearing left on the avenue Daumesnil, there is a series of brick archways under a bridge that carried the now abandoned railway. The viaduct was renovated in the 1980s to become an elevated park, called the *Promenade Plantée*, where one can walk for miles among shrubs and flowers without descending to the street. On the

Opéra Bastille

ground level it is called the Viaduc des Arts, for the shops installed in the arches below. Preference was given to artisans, such as luthiers, rug weavers, art restorers and other crafts. Beneath one arch is the

Promenade Plantée

Viaduc Café, a pleasant stop for coffee or lunch. This conversion of an elevated railway to a promenade was a prototype for other cities, most recently the high line walkway in New York City.

The No 8 will take you back to the Ecole Militaire stop or better yet, take my all-time favorite bus and either relax and enjoy the sights or stop at places of interest on the way back.

THE NUMBER 69 BUS

The legendary No 69 bus is celebrated in frequent newspaper and magazine articles. There is even a YouTube video of its route on the internet. The bus runs between Gambetta and the Champs de Mars which is in front of the Ecole Militaire, where we started out. The ride in the direction of the Champs de Mars is the famous one. The bastille stop is at the corner of the rue St-Antoine and the Place de la Bastille. The stops for the two directions are across the street from each other. Gambetta, the last stop in the eastern direction is next to the Père

No 69 Bus

Lachaise cemetery, so if you are keen to join throngs of fans paying their respects to the tomb of Jim Morrison as well as those of Chopin, Balzac, Héloise and Abélard and Oscar Wilde, by all means take the ten minute ride in that direction, and then start the westward journey back across Paris. Otherwise, board the Champs de Mars bus on the corner across the square from the Opera. The bus will travel westerly along the rue St-Antoine through the Marais, an ancient neighborhood whose name means swamp or marsh, its condition before it was settled in the 13th century. Over the next 400 years it would become the most fashionable quarter in Paris, before falling into decay and then rescued again in the 1960s and designated a protected area. It has evolved since then from a starving artist kind of place to a Bohemian-chic, sought after quarter. It has been called "the left bank of the right bank."

RUE DE BIRAGUE–PLACE DES VOSGES

Get off at the first stop, Birague, and take the one block street of the same name on the right. Just ahead is the entrance to the Place des Vosges, thought by many to be the most beautiful square in Paris. It was a jousting ground near a royal residence under King Henri II, who met an untimely end when he was struck in the eye and killed by a broken lance during a competition in 1559. The area sat abandoned until the beginning of the 17th century, when Henri IV began

Place des Vosges

building the square to house aristocrats and high-end artisanal work-shops like silk making. When Henri IV was assassinated in 1610, it fell to his successor, Louis XIII to complete the square, and his statue is in its center. The square became the first known luxury condo development. Today there are galleries and restaurants in the covered walks around the square. Across the square directly opposite the rue de Birague, the rue de Béarn exits the square. If it's time for lunch, take the first right onto the rue Roger Ver-lomme. At the end of the block, under the

Rue Birague to the Place des Vosges

green striped awning sits the delightful Chez Janou, a neighborhood restaurant that evokes Provence and the Mediterranean. Tapenade,

Chez Janou

ratatouille, fresh fish, and dozens of flavors of Pastis all make for a taste of summer year round. On warm evenings the square in front fills with waiting diners enjoying aperitifs. Now go back through the Place des Vosges to the rue St-Antoine and continue to walk west. You will come across an imposing entrance

Hôtel de Sully

Louis XIII, **Place des Vosges**

Hôtel de Sully, Orangerie

St-Paul Clock

St-Paul

13th Century Wall of Philip II Augustus

to an authentic 17th century "hôtel particulier" or private home of the aristocrat, Duke de Sully, the finance minister of Henri IV. Pass into the courtyard to view a château-like residence. Continue through the home into the gardens and the Orangerie, to find the "secret" door that leads right back into the Place des Vosges. The Marais quarter is full of once-abandoned private mansions like this one that have been restored and are open to the public. If time permits, devote a whole day to this remarkable quarter. A lit-

tle further up the rue St-Antoine, turn right on the rue Caron, another one block street. At the end is the Place du Marché St-Catherine, the site of an old market near a former convent of the

Place du Marché St-Catherine

same name. The tiny square is edged in Mulberry trees and lined with outdoor cafés. It has the feel of a provincial town square miles away from Paris. This is a good spot for a coffee or an aperitif.

ST-PAUL

The next bus stop is St-Paul but continue to walk the short distance along the rue St-Antoine. The métro and bus stops here are named for the imposing baroque church of St-Paul-St-Louis completed in 1641. The building was cleaned in 2012 and the flamboyant clock on the façade restored. It is worth going inside just to gaze up at the central dome. The network of streets behind the church is known as the Village St-Paul. It is not a village in the tradition-

al sense but a series of small cobblestoned courtyards lined with antique dealers and cafés. Interspersed around the neighborhood are remnants of the thirteenth century city wall from the reign of Philip II Augustus. One span backs up to a school playground.

Village St-Paul

Hôtel de Ville

HÔTEL DE VILLE

Back on the bus departing from St-Paul, the rue St-Antoine becomes the rue de Rivoli which Napoléon cut through the right bank of Paris and named for one of his military victories. The next stop is the Hôtel de Ville, which means City Hall in French—don't try to get a room there! It's a re-creation of the one destroyed by the angry mob in 1871. Designed in the Renaissance style, it hosts art exhibits and concerts in its salons and an ice skating in winter on its front square. The

BHV

sides of the building hold statues of famous Parisians.

Another landmark (at least to me) and one not found in tourist books is the "everyman's" department store, BHV, or Bazar de l'Hôtel de Ville across rue de Rivoli. Its founder was given a permit in 1856 by Empress Eugénie to build one of the first real department stores in Paris. When we bought our place in Paris, we made regular trips here for kitchen gadgets, chandeliers, and window treatments. My favorite floor is the entire basement, the largest hardware store I have ever seen. I can spend hours there even when I know exactly what I want. It is full of knowledgeable clerks who are happy to give advice on making repairs or home improvements. I bought an electric drill and some towel racks for our bathroom and was warned to drill *doucement* (softly) through the ceramic tile. A friend told me that in the 1960s, BHV was still selling engine and body parts for the legendary Citroën 2CV, the post war "everyman's" automobile.

CHÂTELET - TOUR ST-JACQUES

Back on the bus, continue on the rue de Rivoli to the Châtelet stop. On the left side is the Tour St-Jacques. The bell tower is all that re-

Tour St-Jacques

mains of a sixteenth century church dedicated to St James the Apostle. In French, St James is St-Jacques, and in Spanish, Santiago. Pilgrims once gathered here to start the trek to Santiago de Compostela in Spain where he is buried. The rue St-Jacques starts here and continues across the Seine up through the Latin Quarter on the left bank. It was the road leading south that was followed by the pilgrims. *Coquilles St-Jacques* on a menu in France are scallops on the half shell. Pilgrims would bring

back a scallop shell (coquille) from the sea near the tomb of St-James in Compostela as a souvenir. The way of the pilgrimage was often marked by the sign of the scallop shell.

Coquille St-Jacques

PALAIS ROYAL

As the bus approaches the Louvre on the left, it will stop at the Palais Royal which is on the right. It was built by Cardinal de Riche-

Palais Royal Fountain

lieu, advisor, minister and the man behind the throne of Louis XIII. He was a good money raiser and apparently took a nice cut for himself, funding the arts and letters as well as his own palace. He died in 1642, a few years after its completion. It passed to the king, then to the queen and her young Louis XIV. It was a royal residence off and on, gradually becoming luxury apartments for aristocrats. The area declined after the king moved to Versailles and became a hotbed of gambling, dissent, and general bad behavior leading up to the revolution. Today it is a tranquil place with the arcades housing upscale boutiques and restaurants. Children especially like the modern tree stump like sculptures that they can stand on and pose.

Palais Royal

LE LOUVRE

You definitely want to get back on the bus at the Palais Royal stop because the driver will show his stuff by driving through an arch that is too small right into the courtyard of the Louvre and then stop near the I. M. Pei Pyramid. One can choose to "do" the Louvre, walk in the Tui-

No 69 Bus into the Louvre

leries Gardens or stay on the bus. The Musée du Louvre is immense. It has been said that if one spent ten minutes looking at each painting it would take ten years to see them all, not including the sculpture and cultural artifacts. I personally use a "big three tour" for visitors with short attention spans: the *Mona Lisa*, *Vénus de Milo*, and the *Winged Victory*, with appropriate photo ops at each. Shallow yes, but it's all some

The architect I. M. Pei designed the large glass and metal pyramid. It opened in 1989 as the main entrance

Leonardo da Vinci, *Mona Lisa*, Louvre

"The "big three" most recognized workes in the Louvre"

Vénus de Milo, Louvre   *Winged Victory*, Louvre

people want. There is also a two-hour highlights tour that includes a headset. Spending days on end at the Louvre and other museums is a luxury I now have in retirement. I find it relaxing.

LE MUSÉE D'ORSAY

The bus will cross the Seine via the Pont du Carrousel. At the second stop on the left bank is the Musée d'Orsay. While many cities' urban renewal efforts amount to tearing down the old to build the new, Paris has learned to creatively recycle abandoned relics of the past. Today's Musée d'Orsay was built as a train station, the Gare d'Orsay, during a vibrant period around the turn of the century that spawned its own décor, known as *Fin-de-Siècle*. It was built on the former site of a royal palace, the Palais d'Orsay. The names of the towns that the station served are carved around the top of the exterior. The station was the only one built so close to the city center and on a very small space, wedged in among other buildings. This was the ultimate cause for its obsolescence and closure in 1939. When it was built the

limited technology of steam locomotives made for short trains and the Gare d'Orsay had very short platforms for passengers. As trains became more powerful and longer it just couldn't handle them. All the other Paris train stations

Musée d'Orsay

have wide, covered open-ended terminals. The building sat vacant for many years. It was used for a while as an auction house then slated for demolition in the 1970s. An elegant solution emerged in 1977 when it was decided to house the Louvre's extensive collection of Impressionist art in its own dedicated museum. The Musée d'Orsay houses works by Monet, Whistler, Degas, Renoir, Manet and other colorful examples of the world's most popular art genre. Besides the art itself, the building features two giant glass-faced clocks where visitors can look out from the museum toward Montmartre.

Esplanade des Invalides

ESPLANADE DES INVALIDES

The No 69 will now snake through the narrow streets of the left bank along the rue de Grenelle, which opens up at the Place des Invalides, where to your right is the Pont Alexandre III. The first stone of this Art Nouveau style bridge was laid in 1896 by Czar Nicolas II in honor of his father during a period of Franco-Russian freindship. It was one of a series of projects designed to show off Paris for the Universal Exhibition of 1900. The bridge's gilded statues and graceful curves have appeared in paintings and movies, most recently Woody Allen's *Midnight in Paris*. It leads the way from the right bank into the park-like Esplanade des Invalides, one of the few lawns in Paris where soccer games are tolerated. Across the river is a glass structure, the Grand Palais, facing the smaller Petit Palais, both built for the 1900 exhibition. The bus continues on the rue de Grenelle to the Champs de Mars where it makes its final stop in front of the Eiffel Tower.

Pont Alexandre III and Grand Palais

Gare de l'Est

TRAINS

In France all roads literally lead to Paris—railroads that is. Outside of the Paris area it is nearly impossible to go from one region in France to another without changing trains in Paris, sort of like if Washington, DC, were the only airline hub in the US (except in France everyone *wants* to go to Paris). France was a late bloomer in rail transportation. The U.S. had operating lines in the Northeast by 1830. England started a decade earlier. In the 1840s, separate rail lines were built to reach the frontiers of France from Paris. In addition to allowing Parisians the luxury of day trips to the countryside, the rail network ushered in a wave of immigration from the distant provinces at a time when France was a country in name only. In 1920, over 50 percent of the population of Paris was made up of immigrants born in the provinces. Bretons, Bordelais, Auvergnats, and Alsaciens among others were deposited at one of the grand terminals in Paris that served their region, bringing their food, customs, and dialects to the potpourri that makes Paris great. The neighborhoods around stations were the most convenient and hospitable places for new immigrants to find friends and relatives, as well as living quarters and jobs. Today the neighborhoods still reflect the influence of regional immigration. Alsacian brasseries around the Gare de l'Est, serve *choucroute garni* and mugs of beer. On the rue du Montparnasse, near the station of the same name, no fewer than eleven crêperies can be found serving brown ham and cheese filled crêpes washed down with bowls of sparkling cider. The area is known as Little Brittany. Our favorite crêperie is Josselin, authentic

Crêperie Josselin

down to the Breton lace lampshades. The Gare St-Lazare, Paris' first,

Claude Monet, *The Gare St-Lazare*, Fogg Museum, Cambridge Mass

with trains from the north, was captured in paintings by Manet, Caillebotte, and Monet. Its surrounding streets are still rife with oyster sellers from Normandy. Across from the entrance to the Gare d'Austerlitz is the Relais d'Auvergne, named for the region served by the station. The Gare du Nord, the traditional arrival spot from Northeast France and Belgium faces the Art Déco Terminus Nord restaurant that serves up platters of North Sea crustaceans. It is the Gare de Lyon, however, that stands out as a temple of luxury dining. Built at the time of the Universal Exhibition of 1900, along with the Grand Palais and the Pont Alexandre, it focused on getting wealthy British travellers from Paris to the Mediterranean resort towns of Nice and Monte-Carlo, but not before they dined at its restaurant, Le Train Bleu. It bills itself as the best preserved and

Relais d'Auvergne near Gare d'Austerlitz

most stunning example of Belle Epoque style in Paris. One dines under a vaulted ceiling covered with murals and gold leaf. Paintings of Côte-d'Azur ports grace its walls and crystal chandeliers illuminate the palace-like hall. Recently, the level of service appears to have deteriorated, but the best part is still the décor.

Gare d'Austerlitz

Le Train Bleu, Gare de Lyon

Railway stations in Paris today have entered the age of the *Train à Grande Vitesse* (TGV) that cruises at 200mph. One train recently set a noncommercial speed record of over 350mph. These trains make driving and even flying within Western Europe appear slow and obsolete. A few hours will take you to Amsterdam, London (via the Chunnel), or Frankfurt; even less to cities

Les TGV, Gare de Lyon

in France, all downtown to downtown with no airport taxis, security lines, or hassles. Paris Charles de Gaulle Airport has itself become a major rail hub with nonstop TGV connections to major cities in France and the rest of Europe.

BOATS

Boats have been integral to Paris from even before it was Paris. Dugout canoes found just west of the city date back over 4000 years. They can be seen today in the Musée Carnavalet in the Marais. Around 200 BC, the Celtic Parisi people, skilled boaters, settled on what is now the Ile de la Cité, using the surrounding Seine as their moat. When the Romans arrived around 500 years later, they did the same. The island also served as a prime spot for crossing the Seine, sort of a land-water crossroads. If the island is the center of Paris, Paris is considered to be the center of France, in importance

Paris Emblem

if not in geography. The zero mile marker for all of France can be found on the Ile de la Cité, right in front of the Notre-Dame Cathedral. The stone prow at the tip of the Ile de la Cité that appears to cut through the Seine is perfect symbolism of Paris as a ship. The city's coat of arms is based on that of the boatman's guild which can be traced to Roman times. Adopted by

Charles I in the 12th century, it shows a ship on rough water beneath a pattern of fleur-de-lys. The city's motto, inscribed below in Latin, reads *Fluctuat nec murgitur*, meaning "It is tossed by the waves but does not sink." Yet another icon of the city as a boat can be seen in the stand-alone historical markers throughout the city. They are in the shape of an upside down medieval canoe paddle.

Midieval Canoe Paddle

Today there are two main types of boats on the Seine, the *péniche* or self-propelled work barge and the tour boat, popularly known as a *Bateau Mouche*, which is actually a brand name but sometimes used generically to describe the double deck floating cruisers with headphones and running commentary. Every first time visitor to Paris rides them. The closest tour boats to our neighborhood leave from the wharf at the foot of the Eiffel Tower. Based at the same wharf but

Bateau Mouche

at the other end of the spectrum are the Bateaux Parisiens, where elegant dinners are accompanied by live musicians while cruising past floodlit landmarks. They depart at 8:30 each evening. It's classy and perfect for romantic occasions.

Canauxrama operates a unique cruise from the Arsenal Marina near the bastille along Canal St-Martin for a two and a half hour ride. The canal goes underground halfway up its three mile length and then

Canal St-Martin Canauxrama tour

opens up into a scenic waterway beneath a canopy of hundred year old plane trees. Watch the workings of the locks as they gradually lift the boat to the level of the Bassin at La Villette where it meets a canal from the River Ourcq.

In New York, it would be called a water taxi, but in Paris it is the Batobus. They cruise up and down the Seine in central Paris and are

Batobus

"hop on-hop off" unlimited use, with one day passes at fifteen Euros and five days at twenty-one Euros. Each of its eight stops is on a quay of the Seine near a major attraction: the Eiffel Tower, the Musée d'Orsay, Notre-Dame Cathedral, the Hôtel de Ville, the boulevard St-Germain, the Louvre, the avenue des Champs-Elysées, and the Jardin des Plantes, where the Natural History Museum can be found. The only drawback is the stairs that must be climbed from the wharf to the sidewalks.

If you are young enough to climb the stairs, you are probably young enough to go partying at night, and the Batofar is the place to be. A converted lighthouse ship from Ireland, its name is a cute French phonetic contraction of *bateau-phare*, the word for lightship. It is hip,

Batofar

or as the French say, *branché,* opening at 8:00 pm and going all night on weekends with live "electromusic" and DJ's. For us non night-hawks, there is a Sunday brunch. In the summer there is also a bar open on the dock, called the Batofar Beach. To get there take the No 6 Métro to quai de La Gare.

Menu du Jour

Entreé + Plat : 18€
Plat seul : 13€

Entrée : Velouté Dubarry, Chorizo, huile de noix

Plat : Risotto, ballotine de volaille et bisque mousseuse

LES ENTREES 5,00€

- Celeri Rémoulade
- Assiette de charcuterie
- Assiette de crudités
- Avocat au Thon ou aux Crevettes
- Oeuf Dur Mayonnaise
- Harengs Pommes à l'huile
- Poireaux Vinaigrette

LES PLATS 11,00€

- Petit salé aux Lentilles
- Escalope de dinde Normande. P. Vapeur
- Entrecôte, Haricots Verts - 18€

LES DESSERTS 5,00€

- Mousse au chocolat
- Crème Caramel
- Compote de pommes
- Gâteau de Riz
- Charlotte aux poires
- Oeufs à la Neige

de Menu Corse...
28,00€

- Planchette de coppa
- Civet de Sanglier, Polenta
- Planchette de Brebis
   ou dessert au choix sur l'ardoise
- Un verre de vin Corse

CE MIDI

NOS SALADES 11,5€
CHÈVRE, CAESAR, PAYSANNE.

PLAT DU JOUR 14€
PAVÉ DE THON, ECRASÉ DE POMME DE TERRE. SOJA, CARAMEL.

CARPACCIO DE BOEUF. 12,4€

Plat du Jour 9,50€
FORMULE 12€

- melon Jambon
- Salade de Lentilles
- Ass de Crudités
- Terrine de Campagne
- Hareng P. à l'huile

- Saucisse de Sanglier Purée
- Blanquette de Veau, Riz Basm.
- Rosbif Tagliatelles
- Aile de Raie P. Vapeur

CHAPTER 3

Eating and Drinking–
Food, History and Literature

s I was walking along the rue Cler, I passed the neighborhood grade school and its glassed-in bulletin board. What caught my eye was the school lunch menu for the following week, I should say menus—each day was different. The one for *jeudi* (Thursday) read:

Carottes vinaigrette

Tomates aux olives

Cuisse de poulet basquaise (Basque chicken)

Petits pois à *l'étuvée* (Sauteed peas)

Petit Moule (Cheese from Brittany)

Chèvre (Goat cheese)

Gâteau au chocolat

This is what they are feeding school children! A four course lunch: entrée, main course, cheese course and dessert. I'll bet they are also being schooled on proper table manners. No pizza or hot dogs for these little gourmands. They are learning how to appreciate the art of eating well. These daily menus could have appeared in any good neighborhood restaurant. This is one way the French perpetuate the world's most renowned food culture. Start 'em young!

For visitors, every neighborhood in Paris has multiple categories of dining options. The nomenclature: restaurant, brasserie, bistro, café, bar à vin, salon de thé (pronounced "tay"), can cause confusion. Some places, hoping to cast as wide a net as possible, put all the names on their awning. In their purest form however, each has a place in the history of food in Paris, and can still be enjoyed today in their original style.

THE RESTAURANT

The word restaurant comes from *restauration*, or the restoring of strength. Originally, consommé or beef bouillon was sold on the street as a restorative for weary or sick people. The common folk did not have kitchens of their own. Roasters and sellers of meat were regulated by the city. Before the revolution, there were no sit-down restaurants with chefs as we know them today. The only public place to get a meal, and then not a very good one, would have been as a guest of an inn. But we owe the existence of restaurants to the sybaritic lifestyle of the royalty, when nothing was too exquisite to serve at Versailles and in the salons of Parisian aristocrats. (Remember "Let them eat cake"?) There were guilds and apprenticeships that assured a steady supply of masters of the kitchen. Although many of the royals were executed during the revolution of 1789, the cadres of royal chefs and their staff were spared. Out of work, they began hosting fancy dinners on a commercial basis to those who could afford them. Despite the migration of chefs to the private sector, something was still lacking in the development of a restaurant culture. At Versailles, cost was not a factor and chefs were not running businesses. Hundreds of dishes, appetizers, main courses of every kind of fish and meat, desserts and pastries were prepared each day and set out for the royals to choose from at their leisure. There was no order to the meal. Kitchens didn't need to be very organized or efficient. This costly and wasteful banquet model didn't work well as a private enterprise. A new system was needed. A man

Auguste Escoffier

named Marie-Antoine Carême developed it. Trained as a baker, he impressed Napoléon who had him design a year's worth of non-repeating menus for the state dining rooms using seasonal ingredients. Carême classified sauces and, most importantly, introduced the serving of individual courses in order instead of buffet style. Later, Auguste Escoffier continued the regimentation by developing today's modern kitchen "brigade", a hierarchy with *chefs, sous chefs, sauciers, rôtisseurs*, and even *plongeurs* (dishwashers). Although he and Carême have each been called "the king of chefs and the chef of kings", Escoffier is the better known of the two. He became an international celebrity chef, opening a cooking school in Paris and publishing the first French culinary guide. A great example of the post-revolutionary style dining rooms is Le Grand Vefour, in a corner of the Palais Royal. The décor is neoclassical, the food

Le Grand Vefour

is textbook French, and the service is impeccable. The focus of the attention is on you as an honored guest. The banquettes have brass plaques honoring Honoré de Balzac, Victor Hugo, Joséphine Bonaparte, and other former regulars.

Generally, a restaurant will serve only lunch, usually until 2:00pm, and dinner starting around 8:30pm. It will not have a bar. There will be a daily menu, a selection of dishes that changes with the seasons. It will include an *entrée* (always the first course in France), *a plat principal*, or main dish, and a dessert, all at a *prix fixe*. A cheese course may be ordered before or instead of dessert. Even at the grandest restaurants, the fixed price menus are usually the best value. On the other hand, one can order à *la carte* from a selection that may not change daily or seasonally. The more local and the better the restaurant, the later it starts serving and the more important to reserve in advance. The French consider cuisine to be part of their national patrimony and go to great lengths to protect it. Places of origin of cheeses, sausages, chickens, cuts of meat, and just about everything on the dinner table are registered and tightly regulated. Legislation has even been proposed to restrict the use of the name "restaurant" to establishments that cook everything from raw materials on the premises.

THE BRASSERIE

The French word *brasserie* means brewery. Brasseries originated in Alsace, a region of France that borders the Rhine River. Alsace has been annexed by Germany several times in history, but was won back after each of the world wars. The half-timbered houses, Riesling wines, local beers, the renowned *choucroute garnie*, (a French version of sauerkraut), and a fair amount of Teutonic kitsch give Alsace a de-

Choucroute Garnie

cidedly German feel. But be careful about saying so when visiting, because the locals are quite prickly about even the slightest hint of comparison to Germans. Alsacians are extremely patriotic and are quick to point out that the French national anthem, "La Marseillaise", was written in Alsace. In Paris, brasseries are legacies of migration from Alsace in the 1860s, but beer is no longer brewed in any of them. A genuine brasserie serves Alsacian food, wine, and draft beer. The dish they all have in common is *choucroute garni*. Essentially, it's sauerkraut, which has all the sourness rinsed out of it, cooked in Riesling wine and served on a heaping platter with potatoes, smoked pork chops, sausages, and pigs knuckles. It is big food! It's also fairly low priced considering the quantity and quality. Parisians love it. Bofinger, (pronounced Bo-fan-zhay), just off the Place de la Bastille, is the ultimate brasserie. It's full of Belle Epoque and Art Nouveau décor and has a magnificent domed skylight. Beware! Today, many places that put the word brasserie on their signs do not serve Alsacian food at all. It just means they have draft beer.

Brasserie Bofinger

THE BISTRO

In the folklore of food, there are several versions of the origin of the bistro (sometimes spelled bistrot but pronounced the same). My favorite one has to do with taxi drivers. Whichever country is currently riding the wave of immigration in a city can usually be determined by the nationality of the taxi drivers. In Paris it was the Russians fleeing the revolution of 1917. No one knows better than taxi drivers that time is money; and when they took a lunch or dinner break, the Russians would shout, "*Bistro, bistro*" ("Quickly, quickly" in Russian) to the waiter. A place that served a low cost plat du jour, prepared in the morning and served all day without delay, became known as a bistro. Today, some neighborhood places still fit that mold. Classic, genuine bistros that evoke old Paris are very popular, but are no longer fast or cheap. Allard and Paul Bert come to mind. Their food is classically simple: lamb stews, coq au vin, roasted chicken. Think garlic! Several bistros have been acquired by celebrity chefs

Bistro Le Jean Bart

that try a little too hard to be unpretentious and genuine, but bistro food seems to have migrated everywhere from Paris.

THE LAST BOUILLONS

The first bouillons opened in the Mid-Nineteenth Century, to feed as many workers as possible in *Les Halles*, the central market that Emile Zola called "the belly of Paris." A butcher created a simple dish, pieces of beef in beef bouillon. Served and consumed quickly, it was an ideal meal break for workers to restore their energy. Their appeal spread and by the turn of the century, several hundred could be found across the city, with the newer and pricier ones sporting Art Nouveau and Belle Epoque décor. The menus expanded but remained simple and soon all classes of Parisians were indulging in the latest craze. Over the years just about all of the bouillons were re-incarnated into other genres of restaurants. Vagenende, a brasserie on the boulevard St-Germain was part of a chain of bouillons. It opened in 1904. Its Belle Epoque style reigns throughout the dining room. Mirrors, warm woodwork, and chandeliers act as a time machine. The menu is traditional, but upscale—as is its clientele. Only two places in Paris are still considered authentic bouillons. They are opposites in terms of décor and demeanor. The Bouillon Chartier on the rue du Faubourg-Montmartre, founded in 1896, has that blue collar we-are-all-in-this-together-feel that I love. Upon entering, one is

Bouillon Chartier

struck by the sheer size of the room. It's more like a dining hall, two stories high with a surrounding balcony for overflow seating. Brass coat racks and shelves for whatever customers are carrying line the rows of tables. A glass ceiling, tall mirrors, and dark varnished wood amplify the kind of good noise that comes with lunching with family, friends, and colleagues. Larger tables are shared with strangers during peak hours. Wooden cabinets with small numbered drawers are built into the walls. These once held cloth napkins for regular customers who would go to their numbered drawer and take out their napkin, then put it back when leaving. Once each week all napkins would be washed and returned to the drawers. This practice was ultimately outlawed as unsanitary, but the drawers remain. The waiters sport black, multi pocket vests with long white aprons, which along with their brusque (but friendly) manner makes them appear as right out of central casting. They scrawl your order on the paper tablecloth. The food they bring from the kitchen is charged to them and they have to settle up at the end of their shift, giving them ample incentive to collect from the customers, making change from their large vest pockets. Working class daily specials such as veal kidneys in mustard sauce may put off some people, but the menu itself is expansive as well as inexpensive. There are over a dozen starters costing between one and four Euros each, such as a tomato salad, celeri remoulade, and poireaux (leeks) vinaigrette. The main courses include roasted farm chicken with frites, choucroute alsacienne, sea bass with fennel, grilled lamb and veal, all priced at ten to thirteen Euros. Chartier is filled for lunch every day. My American habit of eating lunch at around 12:30 allows me to avoid the lines that began to form outside at 1:00 each day.

At the other side of central Paris on the left bank sits the Bouillon Racine on the rue Racine. It dates from 1906, near the apex of the short-lived Art Nouveau movement. It was also a time when bouillons were moving upscale and the Bouillon Racine became an Art Nouveau palace with all the hallmarks: flowery chandeliers, beveled mirrors, mosaics, gold lettering, and paintings in the style of Alphonse Mucha, all framed by the pale green ironwork that characterizes the mouvement. We tried it because of the period décor that was painstakingly restored in 1996, but we were more than delighted by the quali-

Bouillon Racine

ty of the food: delicate offerings of asparagus velouté and baked cod with Swiss chard. Lunches here tend to be longer lasting as basking in the ambience is part of the experience. The Bouillon Racine is definitely worth many return trips.

THE SALON DE THÉ

When the subject of tea is discussed, China, Japan, or England usually comes to mind. But in Paris, tea drinking is hardly the pedestrian "cuppa" that exists in England. In the mid-1600s, Louis XIV chartered expeditions to Asia that returned with tea, silk, and porcelain. Afternoon teas became the rage among the aristocrats in Paris years before tea appeared in England. A virtual monopoly was held by the Mariage family who were involved in the first Asia expeditions. Today *Mariage Frères* is one of the world's finest purveyors of

Mariage Frères

tea. Their original tea emporium on the rue du Bourg-Tibourg in the Marais has a quaint salon serving brunch, lunch, and afternoon tea. A two-room tea museum upstairs traces their roots in the China trade. Like restaurants, public tea rooms or *salons de thé*, emerged in the post-revolutionary period. Today there are two general versions. Both types serve light lunches but some also serve breakfast. The grand salons, typified by Ladurée and Angelina's, are elegantly decorated dining rooms and pastry shops. Ladurée started near the Place de la Madeleine in 1862. Its décor reflects the Second Empire. Ladurée

Ladurée

takes credit for inventing the macaron—not to be confused with macaroons. A macaron is an elegant French Oreo, two small round

Angelina

meringues with a sweet filling in between. They come in dozens of flavors and colorful shades. Ladurée's macarons are worshipped around the world. Angelina, on the rue de Rivoli, was founded in 1903 by an Austrian confectioner, Antoine Rumplemeyer. He named it after his daughter-in-law. The tea here is very good of course, but the main attraction is the hot chocolate, made from special African cocoa beans. It's served in pitchers with a side of Chantilly cream. It's so thick and delicious, it will curl your toes. We take first time visitors there for lunch. The other, more numerous, neighborhood tea rooms are less for show and more functional. We often visit them for light lunches. Smart tourists on a budget enjoy the inexpensive but tasty meals featuring salads, quiches, and tarts, and of course good tea or a glass of wine. I still re-

Angelina Chocolate

member the ratatouille tart at a tea room in the Marais. While they attract a lot of "ladies who lunch", tea rooms are always a welcome sight when we are out and about at midday.

THE CAFÉ

The first coffee appeared in Paris in the late 1600s. The source was the Middle East, probably Turkey. It was looked upon as *gauche* by the tea drinking aristocracy, but caught on quickly with the lower classes. It was originally sold via street vendors. An Italian immigrant spice vendor, François Procopio, decided to take coffee upmarket. He opened the Café Procope in 1694. It still exists today on the cobblestoned rue de l'Ancienne Comédie on the left bank. It serves classic dishes in dining rooms from the era of Voltaire, a regu-

Le Procope

lar. From the beginning, the caffeine buzz stimulated conversation, debate, and political theorizing. Marx, Engels, and Trotsky were habitués at Parisian cafés. The intellectual foundation laid in the left bank continued in the Café de Flore and the Deux Magots on the boulevard St-Germain. The café concept spread, and soon Paris had hundreds—now thousands of cafés. The mass market appeal made France a café centered society rather than the British tea culture. Cafés can have grand dining rooms, like the

Café de la Paix near the Opéra, or a few tables and a bar on a corner. Cafés tend to be the common denominator of a neighborhood. The Café du Marché, on the rue Cler near our apartment, opens at seven in the morning. Delivery truck drivers, their overnight shift complete, stand at the bar with a *café calva*, espresso with Calvados, an apple brandy from Normandy. The street cleaners stop by next in their green uniforms. Baskets of croissants are set on the bar for self-service. Newspapers fastened to stick frames are available to share. American tourists arrive seeking omelets. They are told that the kitchen opens at eight. Moms stop by for coffee and chat after walking their children to school. The tables are waited on by a young woman, probably a university student, who brings what you had yesterday without being asked. The retirees wander in later with their dogs. Everyone greets the dogs by name. The cast changes every few hours: office workers having the plat du jour at lunch, friends sharing after work aperitifs, couples having a light dinner around eight, and graduate students from the American university nearby sipping late night mojitos. The daily rhythm doesn't vary much, and this predictability gives a sense of order to the neighborhood. Cafés have unique terminology and customs. For visitors to Paris, it is often cheaper to have coffee and a croissant at a local café than at the hotel, unless breakfast is specifically included in the room rate. The people watching is definitely more interesting at a café. Tourists usually sit at the outdoor tables nearest the sidewalk; Parisians sit at those closest to the café. For coffee drinkers, *"un crème"* (pronounced crem—short for café crème) is like a cappuccino, and usually only consumed in the morning. *Café au lait*, or coffee mixed with hot milk, is something served at home or in the hotel breakfast room, seldom in a café. Asking for one will get you a crème. Ordering *un café* means espresso.

Café du Marché

Then there is *un noisette*, an expresso with cream on the side. (A *noisette* is a hazelnut in French, which describes the drink's color.) American style coffee is *café allongé*. It is essentially an expresso diluted with hot water. *Café décaféiné* will usually be instant coffee. Coffee is always cheaper in a café when served at the bar. The code of politeness suggests that if you want to use a restroom in a café, you should order something.

LE BAR TABAC

There is an in-between kind of place in the realm of eating and drinking that has an even more working class connotation, *le bar tabac*. In France the government has a virtual monopoly on the sale of cigarettes and tobacco products. Tabacs are the licensees. Tabacs also have a concession to sell lottery tickets, postage stamps, and phone cards. They also sell métro tickets, museum passes and batteries. Tabacs are found in every neighborhood and are easily identified by the elongated diamond-shaped orange sign, usually sporting a neon "Tabac." The

sign represents a carrot, which in the old days was placed in the humidors to keep the tobacco from drying out. Some tabacs serve drinks and humble meals and are known as *bar tabacs*, where one can have a glass of wine or brandy at the zinc covered bar and eat a *croque-monsieur*, the French version of a grilled ham and cheese sandwich.

Bar Tabac

Tabac signs in the shape of a carrot

LE BAR À VIN

The wine bar has grown more popular over the years. They usually specialize in one region such as Burgundy, or Beaujolais, and buy directly from the vintners. Oversize wine glasses that hold a third of a bottle have become popular in the US, but have not caught on in France. The French prefer the plain café glasses that are used for wine as well as for water. These smaller goblets allow sampling of several varieties in a wine bar while enjoying a light meal. One of the oldest wine bars in Paris is the Taverne Henri IV on the tip of the Ile de la

Taverne Henri IV

Cité, straddling the Pont Neuf in a 17th century building. It has been there since the 1950s. Sausage, cheese, and sandwiches are served with country wines. A more recent wine bar is *Le Verre Volé* (The Stolen Glass), where the food is of restaurant quality in a rather plain room on the rue de Lancry near the Canal St-Martin. Its wines are not limited to any one corner of France, and the place doubles as a wine store with reasonable prices. I have never encountered wine snobbery in a wine bar in Paris. No one expounds on hints of "wet pencil shavings" or "plummy leather." Maybe the direct link to the soil and sun inspires a quiet reverence for the fruit of the vine and the lack of pretention.

DINING CUSTOMS AND MANNERS

Dining in France can be the experience of a lifetime. Understanding the customs and protocols will make the experience even more memorable. All establishments that serve food or drinks in France are required to show menus in their windows with prices, which include service and taxes. Avoid places with six-language menus in the window (tourist traps?), or at least stay away from those displaying pictures of the food. The French don't drink bad wine. Go ahead and order the house wine, or the wine of the month, by the glass or carafe.

It will be good. If you ask for a *carafe d'eau* with your meal, tap water will be brought at no charge. Parisian tap water is known for its good quality. Ordering *eau minérale* means still or sparkling mineral water (*eau minérale gazeuse*) and you'll be charged for it. A basket of bread will be brought when you order food. It is always included in the price. Your piece of bread is set on the table to the side of the plate, not on it. The waiter will take care of any crumbs before dessert is served. Coffee is always served after dessert, no matter how much you plead for it to be brought at the same time. There is no such thing as a doggie bag; portions are not supersized. Wine, however, is another matter. Diners who do not finish their wine are gladly accommodated with a cork to take the bottle home. (A wine is a terrible thing to waste!) Many corner cafés and bistros advertise "*service continu*", or "nonstop", which means they serve from morning until late at night. They are a good bet for light meals. For picnics in the park, bakeries (boulangeries and pâtisseries) usually sell baguette sandwiches and small ready-to-eat quiches. There is no such thing as a "croissanwich" in France. That is purely an American invention. Eating or drinking

Service Continu

while walking around or on a métro or bus has always been considered *gauche*, although the emergence of Starbucks in Paris is changing the norm, at least for the younger generation. The only exception I've seen is pinching the end off of a baguette and eating it while walking home from the bakery. Everyone seems to do it. The French (and most Europeans) hold the fork in their left hand and the knife in their right hand while eating. You may be tempted to try this in order to fit in. For those who aren't left handed, be careful! It can take years to do this smoothly. I tried to go native once during a business lunch with customers. I dripped sauce on my necktie and nearly stabbed myself in the face. Eating with chopsticks is child's play compared to this.

THE PARISIAN WAITER

Parisian waiters are legendary for both their skill and their sometimes brusque attitude. Above all, they are professionals—even *artistes* in their own way. Servers should be addressed as Monsieur or Madame. Calling a waiter garçon went out with the 60s. The staff of a restaurant moves like a choreographed ballet. Whether a three-star legend or a

small family owned menu-on-the-chalkboard kind of place, waiters will discuss the daily offerings and recommend wine pairings.

Waiters will NEVER:

– Introduce themselves; as in "Hi, my name is Troy (Tiffany) and I'll be your server tonight."

– Ask, "Are you still working on that?" (When I hear that in the US I think of vultures and road kill.)

Parisian waiter at Bouillon Chartier

– Remove one person's plate from the table before all have finished. This has become a common practice in the U.S. It tends to make those still eating feel that they should hurry up and finish.

– Present the check before you ask for it. Just say, "*L'addition s'il vous plaît.*"

– Serve diet ranch dressing on the side. France has a universal salad dressing. It's called *vinaigrette* and is used on green salads and other vegetables. It never overpowers, but you know it's there. It is not served on the side. Vinaigrettes usually involve a combination of champagne vinegar, olive oil, garlic, Dijon mustard, an egg yolk, salt and pepper. My favorite recipe is from *Barefoot in Paris* by Ina Garten, a.k.a.the Barefoot Contessa. Lunch in heaven to me is a warm goat cheese salad with vinaigrette and a glass or two of chilled rosé.

Salade de chèvre Chaud

Waiters will never leave room on the check for a tip. Service and taxes are figured into the prices, but it is customary to leave some change on the table in a café and 5 to 10 percent tip after a great experience in a great restaurant. Any tip should be in cash. Tips cannot be added onto a credit card. While they are appreciated, wait staff do not rely on tips for their livelihood. Good waiters enjoy a level of status seldom seen in the U.S. They are well paid. Their employers know how critical they are to success. I've seen small restaurants operate smoothly with only one talented server in the dining room, taking orders for three or four course dinners, uncorking bottles of wine, and delivering flaming desserts.

Eating in Paris is always to be enjoyed at a relaxed pace. No one rushes diners to "turn over" tables. Smaller living quarters encourage young people to linger at cafés until late in the evening. City living also helps to burn off calories. It's normal or us to walk five miles in a day strolling or running errands. We found that it's good to pace ourselves when dining out. We often share a first course if we know it is large by saying, "*pour partager*." (This is *never* done with the main course.) We try to make either lunch or dinner a salad-only meal, but sometimes succumb to dessert. When we do, we usually order "*un dessert, deux cuill*ères" (one dessert, two spoons). Entering and exiting the métro stations does the job of a stair master, and there are always the 100 steps up to our fifth floor apartment if we eschew the elevator.

FOOD FROM THE EARTH

In the U.S., French food is often characterized as expensive, pretentious, only for the wealthy, or limited to special occasions. Many Americans visiting Paris are intimidated by French menus and end up gravitating to Italian restaurants where the pasta and pizza looks and tastes familiar. French menu guides and even iPhone apps can help, but there is no substitute for trying authentic French dishes. Everyday French meals are based on the concept of *terroir*—from the earth. The French delight in the *cuisine de bonne femme* and *recettes de grand-mère* (the good wife's cooking and my grandmother's recipes). Those who consider escargot pretentious, for example, should learn that on a farm in the old days, the children were always sent out after a rain to gather snails—a free source of protein for the family. Cooking them with butter, garlic, and parsley didn't hurt either. Don't look for a boneless chicken breast in your coq au vin at a Paris restaurant. You are eating a rooster that has been stewed all day in red wine. Using prime cuts of meat will ruin beef Burgundy. It's supposed to be made with the lesser cuts and simmered for hours in wine. Actually, anything cooked all day in wine is probably tasty, and sip-

Les Escargots

ping the wine during the process, à la Julia Child, can sharpen the appetite. One of my favorite meals in Paris is *quenelles de brochet* or pike dumplings. As a former Wisconsin fisherman, I know that north-

Auberge Bressane

ern pike are nearly inedible because of what are called Y-bones throughout the meat, too small to cut out but too big to be safely eaten. The French cook and sieve the meat, and then make dumplings with dough and bake them with a sauce of crayfish, butter, and cream. Heavenly! The common thread in these recipes is the humble farm. There are two places in our neighborhood that epitomize this *cuisine de terroir*. The Auberge Bressane on the avenue de la Motte-Picquet is known for its coq au vin and *quenelles de brochet*. Across the street at Le Florimond, Pascal, the chef, prepares his grandmother's recipe for superb stuffed cabbage and serves foie gras from his family's farm in Corrèze. In the fall, his menu may include venison with chestnut sauce. Laurent, his partner in the restaurant, warmly greets the guests, patiently explains the menu choices, guides the selection of wine, and directs the dining room staff. For dessert, their *millefeuille* à *la vanille Bourbon* is unforgettable.

Le Florimond

The farm tradition also means that nothing goes to waste. *Tête de veau*, a popular dish, means literally calf's head. Tripes, boudin noir (blood sausage), and pigs feet are year round menu choices. An English language review of a Paris bistro specializing in offal carried the headline, "They've got guts!" But classic French cooking doesn't mean that nothing has changed in 200 years. In Paris, as in other major cities around the world, creative young chefs are blending new combinations of ingredients to gently tweak old standards, leading to a new descriptive word: "*bistronomy*", (bistro+gastronomy). The art of cooking in France sometimes almost rises to the level of religion. Every so often there is a revolt against orthodoxy that dictates that classical dishes must follow a formula to the letter. The revolts and resulting reforms are usually called nouvelle cuisine. The term was actually in use in the 1700s, and again when Escoffier began formalizing recipes in the eighteen hundreds. As in religion, yesterday's reforms have become today's orthodoxy. The latest "new style" revolt took place in the 1970s and involved rejection of heavy sauces, excessive complication, and overcooking in favor of using fresh herbs, local ingredients, and lightly steaming fish and game. Some have gone too far with nouvelle cuisine with celebrity chefs adding needless bling in an effort to impress. Avant-garde works for me in art or literature but not in food! I find putting gold leaf on a dessert disturbing, but my wife says it makes her feel special. The check makes me feel special.

EATING AND DRINKING IN THE LITERARY ERA

No writer painted the dining and drinking scene in Paris like Ernest Hemingway did. To most Americans, Literary Paris means Montparnasse in the 1920s, but the neighborhood did not become a Bohemian quarter overnight. As early as the 17th century, students from the Sorbonne hung out among the hills south of Paris that were actually piles of tailings from the limestone mines under the area. The highest pile was dubbed "Mount Parnassus." The area was leveled and developed in the eighteenth century. Still outside the city limits, Montparnasse became a cluster of dance halls, cabarets, and hotels of dubious repute.

The migration of artists from Montmartre to Montparnasse began before the First World War. With the advent of the horseless carriage, the many stables in Montparnasse were abandoned. The stables became ideal artist studios and ateliers at low rents. The first of the Montparnasse cafés, Le Dôme (1898) and La Rotonde (1911), welcomed Picasso, Soutine, Braque, Léger, and Vlaminck on their arrival.

The lost generation of American writers, poets, hangers-on, and misfits began descending on Paris in 1920. Hemingway socialized with Ford Maddox Ford and Gertrude Stein. His friend Ezra Pound introduced him to the poet Ernest Walsh. John Glassco escaped his rich family (but not their wealth) to live the life of a fool with money as recounted in his ribald *Memoirs of Montparnasse*. The lure of Paris for Americans went beyond history, romance, and art. Prohibition had just been enacted and the US would remain dry for thirteen years. The French franc collapsed after the First World War, losing 90 percent of its value and making the U.S. dollar king. But despite the influx of writers scribbling their prose in the boulevard cafés, life in Paris was not a prevalent theme in their works, with the exception of Hemingway. He lived with his wife Hadley and their son Bumby in a cold-water flat in Montparnasse, but they could still afford a housekeeper. As he says in *A Moveable Feast*, "We ate well and cheaply and drank well and cheaply and slept well and warm together and loved each other." (sigh.) In a later chapter he added, "Two people then could live comfortably and well on five dollars a day and could travel." The fact that each of them had trust funds couldn't have hurt either. According to Hemingway, the café life prevailed.

> "Everyone had their private café where they never invited anyone and would go to work, or to read or to receive their mail. They had other cafés where they would meet their mistresses and almost everyone had another café, a neutral café, where they might invite you to meet their mistress and there were regular, convenient, cheap dining places where everyone might eat on neutral ground."

Everyone must also have had a good memory to avoid mixing them up.

Harry's Bar

On the right bank, the literary hangouts were the Café de la Paix and Harry's Bar, mainly because of their proximity to the American Express Agency where expats went to get cash, wired from the U.S., before there were credit cards and ATM's. Hemingway found the right bank pleasant but unaffordable. In an attempt at self-exile, he decided to forgo haircuts since shaggy artists were shunned on the right bank. Most literary references come from the Bohemian left bank. One set of hangouts on the boulevard St-Germain has been called the "golden triangle", because it connected two cafés, Les Deux Magots and Café de

Café de Flore

Les Deux Maggots

Flore, with the Brasserie Lipp across the street. The two cafés became the headquarters of the existentialists in the 1940s. Jean Paul Sartre and Simone de Beauvoir were the power couple of the movement. The other cluster is less of a common thread and more of a zipline down the boulevard Montparnasse past a bar and five cafés. Although Hemingway's fondness for adult beverages could make for a Parisian style literary pub crawl, the cafés serve great lunches, so let's call it a "walkable feast."

The starting point will be 42 rue du Montparnasse. It runs off the Boulevard Montparnasse just east of the Tour de Montparnasse skyscraper. At the corner is Le Falstaff, a pub that has survived from the 1920s by adapting. It still has a dozen beers on tap, but today it has a television sports bar following. Mussels, crêpes, and sandwiches are served. Hemingway and Fitzgerald imbibed here. According to legend, Hemingway instigated a

Le Falstaff

fistfight on the sidewalk with a fellow writer for besmirching his reputation. Have a beer, but avoid the fight and make a right turn back onto the Boulevard Montparnasse, the route Hemingway would have walked from the Falstaff to his apartment past five more literary hangouts. Spaced by one short block, four legendary cafés of the era sit two by two facing each other. On the north side of the boulevard are Le Select and La Rotonde, facing La Coupole and Le Dôme to the south. This proximity caused tough competition for the expatriate dollar. In *The Sun Also Rises*, the main character, Jake Barnes, suspects kickbacks.

> "No matter what café in Montparnasse you ask a taxi driver to bring you to from the right bank of the river, they always take you to the Rotonde. Ten years from now it will probably be the Dôme. It was near enough, anyway. I walked past the sad tables of the Rotonde to the Select."

La Coupole was a late starter in the Lost Generation era. Founded by two fired employees from Le Dôme down the street, it opened its doors in 1927, calling itself "the temple of Art Déco." It set itself apart

La Coupole

from the others with its size (billed as largest café in Paris) and a dance hall. Artists such as Léger and Kisling were recruited to decorate the columns supporting the cupola. Because of its late start, it received less attention in the writings of the 1920s. Its heyday came after the Second World War when movie stars and musicians found it the place to be seen. According to its brochure, the dance hall was known as a place where "mature women attracted artists in need" (and maybe vice versa). In 1988, the original building was replaced by an uninspiring office block containing a new version of La Coupole that mimicked the old one. Today, it's more known for the décor than for the food. Across the street, however, Le Select seems to have been the café of choice among Hemingway's crowd. In *The Sun Also Rises*, only a few chapters take place in Paris, but the Select is mentioned ten times versus three each for the Dôme and the Rotonde, perhaps because it was the first to open all night. The Select remains close to original: simple lines, ochre ceiling, bright lighting, and waiters that look like they were around for the opening in 1923. There is a daily menu, nothing too fancy, but everything is good. Duck confit, beef tartare, Lyonnaise potatoes, and other basic dishes are the norm. Early on, the Select responded to the Americans' need for simple and cheap food to balance the rich French offerings and came up with Welsh rarebit, toasted bread covered in a savoury cheese sauce. (I am reminded of our taking a case of Kraft's Macaroni & Cheese to Hong

Kong as emergency comfort food when we moved there in 1994.) Two years ago, on a visit to Le Select, Didier, the waiter, lamented that new management had discontinued Welsh rarebit several months earlier after almost ninety years. Strangely, on a recent visit it was back on the menu. When I mentioned it to the waiter, he just shrugged as if to say, "C'est la vie!" Down the street, La Rotonde basks the afternoon sun, its tables filled with boulevardiers on a busy corner. It opened in 1911, in time for the artists of Montmartre to establish it as a hangout. It did not always fare well in writing, from Jake Barnes' snub to Hemingway's slur, "I passed the collection of inmates of the Rotonde and, scorning vice and the collective instinct, crossed to the Dôme. The Dôme was crowded too, but there were people there who worked." Hemingway wrote a regular column for the *Toronto Star Weekly* from 1920 to 1924, where he further slammed the Rotonde. In the article, "American Bohemians in Paris", he decried "… the strange-looking and strange-acting breed that crowd the tables of the café Rotonde." He referred to them as "the scum of Greenwich Village, New York … skimmed off and deposited in large ladles on that section of Paris adjacent to the Café de la Rotonde." Nevertheless, everyone seemed to make the rounds nightly, stopping at the Rotonde if for no other reason than to heap scorn upon its patrons. At recent lunch at the Rotonde, I found no strange-acting crowds and a surprisingly good selection of classical French dishes like mussels, leg of lamb, and duck with figs.

Le Dôme, which faces La Rotonde, was the prototype of the boulevard café. It opened in 1898 in a classical angled building where the rue Delambre enters the boulevard de Montparnasse. It is hard to find anything in the literature of the day critical of Le Dôme. Hemingway is said to have first used the term "moveable feast" in their dining room. My high opinion of the Dôme is bolstered by what it has become: a Michelin starred temple of seafood. Polished wood booths pay homage to writers and artists who dined there. It is still a place for "people who work", only now it's for people who work in publishing or banking.

Le Select

Bar américain at le Select

La Rotonde

Le Dôme

The last Montparnasse landmark is set apart from the four cafés in more ways than in distance. It's a five minute walk on the north side of the boulevard de Montparnasse to where it becomes the boulevard de Port-Royal. La Closerie des Lilas is unique in all of Paris. It opened in 1847, and its name evokes the arbor of lilacs that grew in front of it. Today it is secreted behind greenery on all sides. There

La Closerie des Lilas

La Closerie des Lilas

is no bling in its signage, just a modest lighted oval placed above the front entrance. It's as if they know who they are and who their regulars are. Why attract walk-ins with garish neon? Even the outdoor tables are behind the green arbor, suggesting perhaps an ideal place for an afternoon tête-à-tête. In *A Moveable Feast*, it became clear that this was Hemingway's workplace.

"The Closerie des Lilas was the nearest good place when we lived down the rue de Notre-Dame-des-Champs in the top floor of the pavilion in the courtyard with the sawmill, and it was one of the nicest cafés in Paris … I sat in a corner with the afternoon light coming in over my shoulder and wrote in the notebook. The waiter brought me a café crème and I drank half of it when it cooled and left it on the table while I wrote."

He became friends with the waiters at the Closerie des Lilas, many of them war veterans, who would pour him doubles and charge him for singles. The wine drinking French were surprised by all the thirsty Americans demanding hard liquor and mixed drinks. Cafés in Montparnasse responded by inventing "Le Bar Américain" to accommodate them. This disturbed Hemingway. One day when he was drinking with the poet Evan Shipman, he learned that "… the new owners want to have a different clientele that will spend some money and they are going to put in an American bar. The waiters are going to be in white jackets, Hem, and they have been ordered to shave off their mustaches." Hem complained, "They can't do that to André and Jean … Jean has had a mustache all his life. That's a dragoon's mustache. He served in a cavalry regiment." When Hem drank the hard stuff it was usually *Rhum St James*, 90 proof dark rum from Martinique. We still see bottles of it on restaurant tables during dessert. It is served with *baba au rhum*, an ordinary looking brown cake doused in rum. It's customary to leave the bottle on the table for those who want to embellish their dessert. The Bar Américain at the Closerie des Lilas is paneled in warm varnished wood with mosaic floors and the same dark red leather banquettes that are in the brasserie, one of its two dining rooms. The other dining room, the restaurant, is glass walled and looks over the greenery surrounding it. It is expensive. The brasserie is not as expensive but not cheap either. The regular crowd in the brasserie has a literary bent, but in an editor kind of way. At lunch, older, well-dressed couples are shown to the tables they reserved. Tweedy types wearing bow ties (which the French call *un papillion* or butterfly) have discussions using their "inside voices" while enjoying oysters, veal kidneys, steak frites, or grilled lamb. At four o'clock a pianist begins playing old standards. This place is not on the regular tourist routes, although the bartender told me of a group of young Japanese asked him if Ernest Hemingway was in that day. The bartender pointed at a man with a beard and they took his picture. On the corner outside la Closerie des Lilas stands a statue of Marshal Ney in his bicorne hat, waving his sword as if to order a charge. His story intrigued Hemingway. Before Napoléon's exile to Elba, Ney was his most trusted leader. When Napoléon escaped and returned to France, Ney helped the now treasonous Napoléon

Marshal Ney

in his attempted coup. After his defeat at Waterloo in 1815, Napoléon was exiled again, this time to Saint Helena. Ney was executed. Hemingway seemed to sympathize with the ill-fated military man.

> *"Then as I was getting up to the Closerie des Lilas with the light on my old friend, the statue of Marshal Ney with his sword out and the shadows of the trees on the bronze, and he alone with nobody behind him and what a balls-up he'd made of Waterloo, I thought that all generations were lost by something and always had been and always would be and I stopped at the Lilas to keep the statue company and drank a cold beer before going home to the flat over the sawmill."*

Hemingway would sometimes turn left at the corner and walk to the Luxembourg Gardens that surround the palace of the same name. In

Brasserie Lipp

its museum, he "… learned to understand Paul Cézanne better and to see truly how he made landscapes when I was hungry. I used to wonder if he were hungry too when he painted …" He would often continue on to the Brasserie Lipp on the boulevard St-Germain, across from the Flore and the Deux Magots.

> *"It was a quick walk to Lipp's and every place I passed that my stomach noticed as quickly as my eyes or my nose made the walk an added pleasure … I asked for a distingué, the big glass mug that held a liter, and for potato salad. The beer was very cold and wonderful to drink. The pommes à l'huile were firm and marinated and the olive oil delicious."*

The Brasserie Lipp is still a Paris institution with waiters in black ties and a menu of Alsacian specialties, only now it is packed at lunch with well-fed business and government power brokers instead of hungry writers.

In between bouts of hunger, Hemingway ate well and drank well, but not necessarily cheaply when someone else was paying. An elegant menu could be concocted from the choices of food and drink in *A Moveable Feast* and *The Sun Also Rises*:

DÎNER à la HEMINGWAY

– Apéritifs –
Pernod • Campari • Cinzano
Champagne (Mumm's and la Veuve Cliquot)

– Entrées –
Oysters (Portugaises and Marennes-Oléron) • Pommes à l'Huile
Pâté • Salade d'endives • Crabe à la Mexicaine • Cervelas

– Plats Principaux –
Cassoulet • Foie de Veau
Tournedos à la Sauce Béarnaise • Poularde de Bresse

– Vins –
Blancs : Sancerre * Pouilly Fuissé * Mâconnais * Montagny
Rouges : St-Emilion * Beaune * Cahors * Châteauneuf-du-Pape * Fleurie

---

The literary era of the lost generation began its decline with the stock market crash of 1929 that took its toll on trust funds. Prohibition was repealed in 1933. In the same year the lifting of the gold standard in the U.S. drove the dollar back down to a more pedestrian value against the French franc. Americans went home. The era was over. The remaining French intellectuals abandoned Montparnasse for St-Germain during the wartime occupation as German soldiers appropriated their beloved cafés on the boulevard. When Hemingway returned to Paris in the next decades, he stayed at the Ritz. He was famous and rich and no longer hungry. He wrote of the 1920s, "But this is how Paris was in the early days when we were very poor and very happy."

Claude Monet, *The Gare St-Lazare*, Fogg Museum, Cambridge Mass

John Singer Sargent, *Monet Painting*, Tate Gallery, London

CHAPTER 4

Impressionism in Paris– Connecting the Dots

I am not an artist or an art major, but I love art, art museums, art auctions, and even flea markets. We began collecting over forty years ago, starting with traditional landscapes and seascapes. Over time we gained an appreciation for Impressionism, actually closer to a passion in my case. I believe that people carry inside them a kind of tuning fork that vibrates to certain works of art, just like it would to musical notes. Put simply, Impressionism resonates with me. Several years ago, when we began spending each spring and fall in Paris, I was inspired to learn as much as I could about the Impressionists:

What drove them to paint as they did?

What was Paris like during their lifetimes?

Where did they hang out?

Where are the best examples of Impressionist art in Paris today?

I learned that before there was Impressionism, painting was targeted to the educated elite. The classical school of art stressed precision. Scenes were researched. None of the art celebrated ordinary people. But several changes and innovations were occurring near the mid-eighteen hundreds that would lead to a new era:

– The industrial revolution ushered in the concept of *le weekend*, even though it was only one day per week.

– In the 1840s railroads were being built that linked Paris to all of the frontiers of France. This set off waves of migration from the provinces to the city, but also let Parisians take leisurely day trips to the countryside. The first railroad ran north from Paris, from the Gare St-Lazare to Normandy, where the Impressionists would adopt towns along the Seine.

– Eighteen hundred and forty-one saw the invention of oil paint in tubes, enabling artists to easily paint in the outdoors. Renoir said, "Without tubes of paint, there would have been no Impressionism."

– In 1839, Louis Daguerre invented a process that could capture a moment in time on a photographic plate. If precise photographs were now possible, how would this impact the classical school of painting that valued precision?

Camille Pissarro, *Avenue de l'Opéra,* **Rheims Museum of Fine Arts**

– Lastly, Paris was undergoing its greatest modernization in history under Napoléon III and Baron Haussmann. They cut grand boulevards across the city and added monuments and showplaces for world fairs. As it electrified, Paris literally became the city of lights. Much of what visitors see in Paris today dates from the nineteenth century.

A CATALYST FOR CHANGE

While this was affecting how Parisians behaved, an essayist, poet, and art critic Charles Beaudelaire provided the spark for a new order. In his now famous essay, "The Painter of Modern Life", he urged artists to break with the past and to paint what they saw around them, basically, people going about their daily lives. Mary Cassatt painted members of the audience rather than scenes from the opéra they were watching. Degas portrayed ballerinas waiting backstage instead of in their performance. The Impressionists seemed to live the life they painted: weekends in the

Gustave Courbet, *Charles Baudelaire,* **Musée Fabre, Montpellier**

Mary Cassatt, *In the Box*, Private collection

Edgar Degas, *The Wait*, Musée d'Orsay

Claude Monet, *Bathers at la Grenouillère*, National Gallery, Washington DC

Edouard Manet, *A Bar at the Folies Bergères*, Courtauld Institute, London

country, eating and drinking, socializing, nightlife, and family gatherings. Today, fans of Impressionism can connect the dots that represent greatest troves of Impressionist art in Paris as well as the weekend retreats that appear in their paintings, places that can be enjoyed today just as they were in the era.

THE MUSÉE MARMOTTAN MONET

It's fitting that our starting point is the Musée Marmottan Monet. It started out as a hunting lodge for royalty, then acquired as a residence by the Marmottan family in 1882. They donated it and their collection of First Empire paintings and furnishings to the Académie des Beaux-Arts, which opened as the Marmottan Museum in 1934. Then in 1957, the art collection of a physician who treated many of the Impressionists was given to the museum. In 1966 one of Mon-

Musée Marmottan Monet

et's sons donated his father's remaining works, making it the home of the world's largest Monet collection. It was renamed the Musée Marmottan Monet. The most important reason for starting the thread here is Monet's *Impression Soleil Levant* (*Impression of a Sunrise*), be-

Claude Monet, *Impression Soleil Levant*, Musee Marmottan Monet

lieved by some to be the first Impressionist painting, or at least the one that gave its name to the movement When it was first shown in 1874, an art critic who decried it as no better than wallpaper, used the word "impressionists" to ridicule the movement.

A special exhibition hall was created on the lower level. It holds scenes of water lilies painted in Monet's old age that show the progression of the master's deteriorating sight, reflecting his "impressions" over time. The museum's collection includes works by Renoir, Degas, Manet, Gauguin, Sisley, and Pissarro.

Claude Monet, *Nymphéas*, Musée Marmottan Monet

What was once outside the city limits now sits in a well-heeled neighborhood of quiet elegance. To get there take the No 9 Métro to La Muette or the 52, 32, or 22 bus. Across the park toward the bus and métro stops is the restaurant *La Gare,* inside a

La Gare

pretty little station of the *Petite Ceinture,* a long abandoned railway that circled Paris during the time of the Impressionists.

Pierre-Auguste Renoir, *Monet Smoking*, Musée Marmottan Monet

THE MUSÉE RODIN

The next stop doesn't involve paintings but sculpture influenced by Impressionism. While both Degas and Gauguin used sculpture as Impressionist media, one sculptor stands above others and has his own museum, the Musée Rodin. As a sculptor, Auguste Rodin could not access the colors of the Impressionists, but he understood how a scene could exist just for the moment and that irregular textured surfaces could catch light differently than the

Musée Rodin

smooth stone or bronze of the traditionalists. His subjects displayed human emotion as opposed to classical or mythical life. Like our previous stop, the museum is installed in a former private residence, in this case, the Hôtel Biron, where Rodin lived as a tenant and worked in his studio until his death in 1917. It was built by an aristocrat in the Renaissance style around 1730 in a suburb of Paris, the Faubourg-St-Germain, then the city's most fashionable neighborhood where homes could be built in the midst of their own walled gardens. The seven acres of elegant gardens are an integral part of the museum complex. A key feature of sculpture museums is that works can be placed indoors or out. Rodin's most iconic work, *The Thinker*, is

Auguste Rodin, *The Thinker,* **Musée Rodin**

enthroned in the garden where visitors can sit before it and ape the famous pose while being photographed.

In another corner of the gardens is the life-size bronze *Burghers of Calais*, celebrating an act of bravery during a 14th century siege by the

Auguste Rodin, *Burghers of Calais,* **Musée Rodin**

British. They threatened the inhabitants of Calais with starvation unless the town councilors or burghers would present themselves for execution. Six of them did just that. The faces of the burghers show the anxiety and misery they felt as they stood ready to die. They so impressed the British that they were spared in recognition of their courage. Inside the restored rooms of the museum are dozens of masterworks and preliminary models, including the erotic *The Kiss,* which had our junior high school-aged sons staring with open mouths on our first Paris trip thirty years ago. The link to the Impressionists is reinforced by the interspersing of paintings by Renoir, Monet, and Van Gogh among the galleries. On a recent visit with family, we came to a long line at the entrance and decided we would

Auguste Rodin, *The Kiss,* **Musée Rodin**

just visit the garden and avoid the line as the grandchildren were tired. At the ticket office, we were told that young children, mothers, and seniors were free, leaving only my son to pay the one Euro entrance fee. The museum sits next to the eastern side of the Invalides at the end of the rue de Varenne. Take the No 69 bus that stops a block away at the rue de Grenelle, or the Varenne stop on the No 13 Métro, which has a large replica of *The Thinker* on the platform.

Métro Varenne

THE MUSÉE D'ORSAY

A short walk east on the rue de Varenne, then north on the rue de Bellechasse will lead to the Musée d'Orsay. While many cities' urban

Musée d'Orsay

renewal efforts amount to tearing down the old to build the new, Parisians have learned to creatively recycle the abandoned relics of the Past. Today's Musée d'Orsay was built as a train station, the Gare d'Orsay, in 1900. It was constructed in a style that combines *Beaux-Arts* with the turn of the century style known as *Fin-de-Siècle*. The names of the cities served by the rail line are carved around the building's exterior. It was the only station built so close to the city center, and on a very small space, wedged in among other buildings. This was the ultimate cause of its obsolescence and closure. As steam locomotives became more powerful and trains longer, the short platforms couldn't handle them. It sat vacant for many years. It was used as an auction house for a while and then slated for demolition in the 1970s.

Gare d'Orsay Clock

James McNeill Whistler, *The Artist's Mother*, Musée d'Orsay

Pierre-Auguste Renoir, *Country Dance*, Musée d'Orsay

Edouard Manet, *le Déjeuner sur l'Herbe*, Musée d'Orsay

An elegant solution emerged in 1977 when it was decided to move the Louvre's extensive collection of Impressionist art to its own museum. The Musée d'Orsay houses the world's largest collection of Impressionist art with works by Monet, Degas, Renoir, Manet, Whistler, and every other artist of the era. At lunch, diners in the café can look out from the giant glass-faced clocks toward Montmartre. There is a bright Rococo style restaurant on the top floor with moderate prices.

Musée d'Orsay Restaurant

Musée d'Orsay Café

THE MUSÉE DE L'ORANGERIE

The next stop is the Musée de l'Orangerie. Walk across the passerelle Solférino, a pedestrian bridge across the Seine built in 1999 that leads into the Tuileries Gardens, then turn left. The name Tuileries comes from the old clay pits along the river where roof tiles or *tuiles* were produced. The Tuileries Palace stood in front of the open end of the Louvre. It was destroyed in the revolution of 1870. Only two long outbuildings remain, both near the Place de la Concorde. One is the old royal tennis court, the *Jeu de Paume*, which today houses photography exhibits. The building closest to the Seine is the *Orangerie*, where oranges were grown for the royalty in the winter months. In

Musée de l'Orangerie

1927, Claude Monet donated a series of large canvases depicting seasonal scenes of water lilies at the pond in Giverny. They were installed as murals in two rotundas in the Orangerie. These rooms have been called the Sistine Chapel of Impressionism.

Then in the 1960s a large collection of Impressionist and Modern Art was donated to the museum. A spacious downstairs gallery was added in 2006. On display are works by Monet, Renoir, Cézanne, Matisse, Picasso, Rousseau, Sisley, Utrillo, Soutine, and others. A truly intense experience! We usually follow a morning visit with lunch at Angelina, a classic *salon de thé*, or tea room close by on the rue de Rivoli, famous for its best-in-the-world hot chocolate.

The Rotunda, Musée de l'Orangerie

MONTMARTRE

It is now time to go out from central Paris and step into some scenes painted by the masters. In the nineteenth century, villages outside the city walls were popular hangouts for those in search of tax free wine and relaxed rules of behavior. Montmartre was a favorite. At the highest point in today's Paris, it was still an independent village until 1860 when it and fifteen other villages were gobbled up in the city's last expansion. It was noted for its windmills and vineyards as well as artillery batteries that were supposed to protect Paris from invaders, but they were more often than not aimed at the city by revolutionaries. Renoir rented his first studio there. He and Pissarro, Monet, and Cézanne bought their art supplies from Julien Tanguy whose shop was on the rue Clauzel. When they were shy of funds,

Musée de Montmartre

they paid him in art. Tanguy lived at No 10 rue Cortot. His apartment, along with the oldest house in the village and the grounds around it, comprise the Musée de Montmartre. The land was acquired in the 17th century from the Abbey which owned much of the area.

The house was built and the land tilled for gardens and vineyards. Renoir's painting of a girl on a swing uses the gardens as a backdrop.

Pierre-Auguste Renoir, _Girl on a Swing_, Musée d'Orsay

The Museum has a permanent collection of Montmartre memorabilia and rotating exhibits such as the recent one commemorating the "_Chat Noir_" cabaret that flourished in the hilltop village in the "gay nineties." Reproductions of paintings adorn the grounds, showing the rural life that you become a part of. In 2014, the former studio and apartment of Suzanne Valadon and Maurice Utrillo were renovated in an adjacent building that now houses the Café Renoir. The museum and its gardens and vineyards seem to deny the proximity to the cliché ridden Place du Tertre where generations of restaurateurs and portrait artists have hustled tourists. The north side of the hill is the more authentic one where the musée, as well as the celebrated artists' hangouts, can be found. Below the vineyard can be seen the "_Au Lapin Agile_", or nimble rabbit, the favorite cabaret of artists over the years from Impressionists to Cubists who discussed the meaning of art between

Le Chat Noir

drinking and singing sessions. An 1875 painting by André Gill shows

Suzanne Valadon Studio

the nimble rabbit jumping out of the stew pot holding a bottle of wine. The stone building sits on a cobbled street. The wooden tables and benches are filled most nights with revelers singing century old French songs. Don't be shy about going in. Everyone is welcome, even if they don't know the tunes.

Montmartre Vineyard — Every year this "secret" vineyard hosts the Montmartre Wine Harvest Festival

Au Lapin Agile, a noisy Montmartre cabaret since 1875, with two shows every night

Le Lapin Agile

Pierre-Auguste Renoir, *Bal du Moulin de la Galette,* Musée d'Orsay

A few blocks away, on the rue Lépic, one of the two remaining windmills in Montmartre stands over the restaurant known as the Moulin de la Galette. The moulin, or windmill, ground wheat that was made into galettes or small bread loaves. In 1830, the owners started

Le Moulin de la Galette

a dance hall that served wine in the surrounding lighted gardens. Its depiction by Renoir in his *Bal du Moulin de la Galette* is one of the most recognized Impressionist works. A smaller twin of the painting sold for a record price at auction in 1990. The dance hall also appears in paintings by Dufy, Utrillo, Picasso, and Toulouse-Lautrec. We recently had lunch in the restaurant under the old windmill. There is no longer dancing, but the food is good and reasonably priced and locals populate nearly all of the tables at lunchtime.

The No 80 bus runs from the Ecole Militaire to the stop at Mairie du 18e-Jules Joffrin, the end of the line. From there a small bus, the Montmartrobus, runs up the last part of the hill to the Place du Tertre.

ILE DE LA GRANDE JATTE

A short bus ride from central Paris will let you visit another favorite hangout of the Impressionists on the Ile de la Grande Jatte. Start by taking the No 82 bus in the direction of Neuilly-Hôpital américain. The bus runs between the Luxembourg Gardens and the American Hospital in Neuilly, a wealthy suburb on the edge of Paris. It stops at the Ecole Militaire bus stop. The bus crosses the Seine from the Eiffel Tower, and then cruises through the 16th Arrondissement. Get off at the last stop before the end of the line at Bineau-La Saussaye. Walk north a

La Guinguette de Neuilly

block, cross the bridge to the island, and look for the red awnings of a restaurant to the right. It is impossible to separate the Impressionists'

Rowers near La Guingette

weekends from the *guinguettes* or riverfront eating and drinking places that sometimes included music and dancing. That's why the Guinguette de Neuilly is an ideal place for lunch. Its two riverfront terraces are ideal for watching the rowers and fishermen. You will feel carried back to the 1890s as you enjoy a leisurely meal. The eclectic modern homes nearby on the Seine remind me a bit of Seattle, and the houseboats moored along the river add to the Bohemian feel. Walk

around the island neighborhood along the boulevard Georges Seurat. Its namesake is best known in the art world for his 1884 Pointillist painting *A Sunday Afternoon on the Ile de la Grande Jatte*, which inspired the modern musical *Sunday in the Park with George*. It now hangs

Georges Seurat, *Sunday Afternoon on the Ile de la Grande Jatte*, Art Institute of Chicago

in the Art Institute of Chicago. There is a small park named after Seurat which leads down to a river walk. A plaque commemorates him and the other Impressionists who came here to paint and enjoy life on the Ile de la Jatte.

ILES DES IMPRESSIONISTES

A little further out from the city, but sill close enough to go for lunch and a stroll is a place called the *Iles des Impressionistes*, along the

Chatou

Seine in the town of Chatou. It was countryside in the time of the Impressionists, who gathered with family and friends for drinking, eating, dancing, bathing, boating, and of course painting. The Hôtel Fournaise was one of their hangouts. When Renoir decided to paint a large-scale canvas to show off his talent, he persuaded friends to gather as they would on a Sunday boating afternoon, dining on the terrace of the hotel. They spent many Sunday afternoons posing, with some dropping out and others taking their places. The result is the *Déjeuner des Canotiers*, or *Luncheon of the Boating Party*. A copy of the 1881 painting stands near the restaurant. The fourteen diners are all Monet's contemporar-

ies and are identified in the literature of the painting. One of them became his wife—I won't tell you which. Try to guess and then look it up. And now for the best part: the Hôtel Fournaise is still there and so is the same balcony where, under an

Pierre-Auguste Renoir, *Luncheon of the Boating Party,* **Phillips Collection**

exact duplicate of the same awning, you can have lunch and dream of those afternoons. The restaurant, called the Maison Fournaise, attracts corporate types from nearby offices, so be sure to reserve ahead. There are boat rides in the summer. A small adjoining museum sells straw

boating hats. For fanatics of the genre I recommend Susan Vreeland's novel, *Luncheon of the Boating Party.* The famous painting now hangs in the Phillips Collection in Washington, DC. We will find out later how some of the world's best French Impressionist art ended up in the

Maison Fournaise

U.S. To get to Chatou, take the Number 1 Métro to La Défense, then buy a ticket on the RER A1 to Rueil-Malmaison. Take the station exit for Albert 1er, go right along the roadway to the bridge, and cross it. The hotel is down on the right.

GIVERNY

Our final taste of Impressionism is the most colorful of them all: Claude Monet's home and gardens in the village of Giverny. It is not easy to get there directly by train—you would need to take one to the town of Vernon, then catch a local bus, so I would suggest a half day bus tour from Paris, which is offered by Paris Visions, leaving at 1:30 pm and returning at 6:00 pm during the week, and on Sunday leaving at 8:30 am and returning at 1:00 pm. The months of May thru September are best for showing

Monet's Home at Giverny

off the irises and water lilies around the Japanese footbridge. Monet bought his farm at Giverny after the death of his first wife and his remarriage. The blended family had eight children. He had the lily pond dug and added the Japanese bridges. A team of six gardeners assured that flowers would be in bloom eight months of the year, specifically

for him to paint. The interior of his modest country manor house is another study in color with some rooms as well as their contents painted in bright blues and yellows. The Paris Visions tour includes a visit to the Giverny Museum of Impressionisms. The odd use of the word stems from its focus on all aspects of Impressionism—its history,

Footbridge at Giverny

themes, and the spread to other forms of art and

design. It is managed by a partnership with the Musée Marmottan Monet, the Musée d'Orsay, and the Monet foundation. It has no permanent art collection but exhibits works from other institutions. A recent show featured the postimpressionist, Maximilien Luce. The museum encourages artists to

Pond at Giverny

come and paint in the beautifully landscaped grounds. There is a *café-salon de thé* (tea room) where light lunches are served on a terrace overlooking the garden.

FRENCH IMPRESSIONISM BACK HOME

Paris may have the best known museums of Impressionism, but the U.S. holds the honor of being the country with the most and some

say the best Impressionist works. There is a reason for this. During the Impressionist era, the institutions of France and the rest of Europe were cool if not hostile toward Impressionism. It was largely uncollected and vastly underappreciated. Its reputation as "outsider art" was exemplified by its popularity among Americans living in or visiting Paris. Gertrude Stein, who built a collection in the

Pablo Picasso, *Gertrude Stein*, Metropolitan Museum

early 1900s, held court at her flat on the rue Fleurus advising visiting Americans on acquisitions. American women in particular deserve our gratitude for their patronage of Impressionism both as individuals and for their influence over their wealthy industrialist husbands who told them to "buy whatever you like" during their trips to Paris. The first American artist to join the Impressionists in France was Mary

Cassatt, who counseled the folks back home to buy as many Impressionist works as possible, one of the best insider tips of all time. Still, Americans abroad were seen by Parisians as crass, nouveau riche who let their money do the talking and liked to buy in bulk, bordering on compulsiveness. But only in America could so many sons of the working class rise to captains of industry and have the foresight to bring Impressionist art back to their home towns during an era when the old-money pedigreed families in the U.S.

Mary Cassatt, *Self Portrait*, Metropolitan Museum of Art

continued to collect old masters. Some of these Impressionist collections have since been dispersed by estate sales, but several have transformed American museums into world class institutions.

Henry Havemeyer was a sugar refining baron whose wife Louisine travelled frequently to Paris and always returned with a load of paintings, heavily weighted toward Degas and Monet. In 1929, almost 2000 works from all genres in their collection were given to the Métropolitan Museum in New York, including Monet's iconic *Bridge over a Pond of Water Lilies*. Years later, the National

Claude Monet, *Bridge over a Pond of Water Lilies*, Metropolitan Museum of Art

Edouard Manet, *The Railway*, National Gallery of Art, Washington DC

Claude Monet, *Railway Bridge at Argenteuil*, Philadelphia Museum of Art

Edgar Degas, *Woman Bathing*, Hill-Stead Museum, Farmington CT

Gallery in Washington was given Manet's *The Railway* from the collection. John G. Johnson, the son of a blacksmith in Philadelphia, became one of the country's greatest business lawyers. He and his wife Ida died childless and left their entire collection including Monet's *Railway Bridge at Argenteuil* to what is now the Philadelphia Museum of Art. Alfred Pope, a partner in the Cleveland Malleable Iron Company and his wife Ada fell in love with Impressionism when they first visited Paris in 1888. Their collection, more known for quality than quantity, included Monet's *Guitar Player*, Degas' *Woman Bathing*, Monet's *View of Cap d'Antibes,* and one of his *Wheatstacks*. Pope retired to his home in Farmington, Connecticut, called Hill-Stead, which today houses the

Claude Monet, three of the six
paintings of *Wheatstacks*, at the
Art Institute of Chicago

Claude Monet, *Water Lilies*,
Art Institute of Chicago

Edgar Degas, *The Millinery Shop*, Art Institute of Chicago

collection in the museum of the same name. Potter Palmer, son of a New York farmer, built a retail empire that became Marshal Fields department store in Chicago and went on to build the luxurious Palmer House Hotel. The Palmer family lifted the Art Institute of Chicago to the first tier of Impressionism in America with their bequest of 1922. Their collection is comprised of eleven Renoirs, several Degas, and twenty-nine Monets, including six of his *Wheatstacks*. Monet painted twenty-five scenes of the same wheat field in different seasons, in different weather, and at different times of day. The six Monet *Wheatstacks* are the cornerstone of the collection. No other museum in the world has more than two of them. The Institute's subsequent purchase of Seurat's *A Sunday Afternoon on the Ile de la Grande Jatte* in 1924 further reinforced its reputation.

Hill-Stead Museum, Farmington CT

Claude Monet, *Grainstacks, White Frost Effect*, Hill-Stead Museum, Farmington CT

Sterling Clark, grandson of and heir to Edward Clark, a founder of the Singer Sewing Machine Company, and his wife Francine put together a collection from 1920 to 1950 that included works by Monet, Sisley, Berthe Morisot, Pissarro, Manet, Toulouse-Lautrec, and both a ballerina painting and sculpture by Degas. They established the

Alfred Sisley, *The Thames at Hampton Court*, Clark Institute, Williamstown MA

Clark Institute in Williamstown, Massachusetts, in 1955 where the collection is housed. A contemporary, Duncan Phillips, grandson of the founder of Jones and Laughlin Steel in Pittsburgh was an educated art critic and collector who bought art with the intention of sharing it with the public. He directed the Phillips Collection in Washington, DC, until his death in 1966. His taste ranged from El Greco to Milton Avery with the Impressionists in between, but the big draw at the Phillips Collection is Renoir's *Luncheon of the Boating Party*. Another Washington institution benefited from an American's largesse. The

National Gallery holds the extensive Impressionist collection of Chester and Maud Dale. Chester began working on Wall Street as a messenger at the age of seventeen and later founded his own brokerage house. He and Maud were late starters in the pursuit of Impressionism, acquiring major works at Paris auctions in the 1920s. Maud, a trained artist, had the eye and ambition to guide their collecting. In 1962 they donated over 300 works to the National Gallery, then still in its formative years,

Pierre-Auguste Renoir, *Girl with a Watering Can*, National Gallery, Washington DC

having only been established in 1941. The collection includes major works by Cassatt, Monet, Cézanne, Matisse, Manet, and Renoir, most notably his *Girl with a Watering Can*. In nearby Baltimore, two sisters, Claribel and Etta Cone, heiresses to a family textile business,

began travelling to Europe in the early 1900s. They became close friends with Gertrude Stein and built a collection of Impressionist and Modern Art that included 500 works by Matisse, and others by Gauguin, Cézanne, Picasso, and Van Gogh. In 1949, this collection was given to the Baltimore Museum of Art and is housed in its own wing. Up in Boston, the Museum of Fine Arts benefited from the largesse of a more patrician crowd. Beacon

Henri Matisse, *Madame Matisse*, Madras, Baltimore Museum of Art

Hill resident John Spaulding, heir to the Revere Sugar fortune, collected with the aim of filling gaps in the museum's Impressionist catalogue. His bequest included the first Cézanne to be shown in the

Claude Monet, *Valley of the River Creuse*, Museum of Fine Arts, Boston

collection. Denman Waldo Ross, a man of independent means and a Harvard professor, donated the first three Monets to the Boston museum, including *Valley of the River Creuse*. The Juliana Cheney Edwards collection includes six Renoirs and ten Monets, including one of his *Wheatstacks*.

Perhaps the strangest tale of American collectors is that of Albert Barnes. The son of a Philadelphia butcher, he worked himself through medical school and then developed a drug that prevented infant blindness caused by venereal disease. By 1912, he was rich enough and still young enough to amass the largest collection of Impressionist art in America. After an exhibit, his collection was ridiculed by the Philadelphia art establishment, then even more snobbish than their New York counterparts. Barnes thumbed his nose at local society and built his

own educational institution in a Philadelphia suburb that opened in 1922. His collection comprised 181 Renoirs, sixty-nine Cézannes, fifty-nine Matisses, forty-six Picassos, and other works by Degas, Monet, Rousseau, Van Gogh, Gauguin, Soutine, Seurat, and Modigliani. That's more Renoirs

Former Barnes Foundation

than in all of the museums of Europe combined. The paintings appeared to be hung on the walls of his galleries haphazardly from floor to ceiling, but it was his way of grouping them by similar use of light, angles, and perspective as a teaching tool. He was active in the school until his accidental death in 1956. But there is a recent twist. Over

Pierre Auguste Renoir, *La famille d'artiste,* Barnes Foundation, Philadelphia

Paul Gauguin, *Haere Pape,* the Barnes Foundation, Philadelphia

Pierre-Auguste Renoir, *After the Bath*, Barnes Foundation

Paul Cézanne, *La Montagne Saint-Victoire*, Barnes Foundation, Philadelphia

Cézanne, *The Card Players*, Barnes Foundation

time, the Philadelphia establishment came to realize the value and importance of what was just down the road and began to look for ways to break Barnes' last will and testament which specified that the collection was to be left as is, right down to exactly how each painting was hung. The city's stated purpose was to make the collection more accessible to the public by moving it downtown. When a series of court cases couldn't dislodge it, a period of financial difficulty at the foundation allowed outsiders to intervene, ostensibly as rescuers, but ultimately shifting control to the Philadelphia Museum of Art. The Barnes Foundation closed its doors in 2011 and reopened a year later in an impressive new building in downtown Philadelphia. The plots, subplots, and alleged double dealings during the last years of the foundation are portrayed in the 2009 documentary, *The Art of the Steal.*

Connecting these dots in the U.S. is obviously a different proposition from in Paris because of the distances, but several institutions in the Northeast are grouped close enough together to visit them by rail. The Washington-Baltimore-Philadelphia-New York-Boston Amtrak Acela train connects five of them European-style by rail without the hassle of airports or driving.

In May of 1990 Renoir's *Bal du Moulin de la Galette* sold at Sotheby's auction in New York for $78.1 million, a new record for an Impressionist work. (See page 116). Then in June of 2008, Monet's *Le Bassin aux Nymphéas* broke that record, selling at Christie's London for $80.5 million. It was a twin of the painting that sold in 1992 for $12 million. The prices reflected the combined popularity and rarity of Impressionist offerings in the market. Unfortunately, these paintings were purchased by private collectors and will possibly never be shown in museums. No other genre of painting has gone from ridicule and exclusion to universal adulation in the space of 100 years.

Claude Monet, *Bassin aux Nymphéas*

Street view, Musée Jacquemart-André

Entrance, Musée Jacquemart-André

CHAPTER 5

How They Lived – Private Homes Open to Everyone

round the end of the nineteenth century, when the arts were flourishing and private wealth was accumulating, prominent families, some of them nouveau riche, built spacious homes in the city and decorated them with the finest art and antiques. Several of the families left their homes and contents to the City of Paris, often with an endowment to maintain them in their original lived-in state, down to the kitchens, servants' quarters, and boudoirs. Other private homes of writers and artists became museums to commemorate their cultural contributions. Not surprisingly, there is a striking difference between the homes of the rich and those of the artists. Writers and artists were generally not born into wealth. Many struggled in their early lives to earn a living. Their homes were more often rented apartments or studios. However, all of the homes-in-to-museums have unique stories, some *romantiques,* some *tragiques.* It is a great opportunity to see how people lived their day-to-day lives. A few homes even incorporate restaurants or cafés. All of them are reachable by métro or bus.

The Musée Jacquemart-André is simply breathtaking, inside and out, but anyone could walk past it without noticing. Hidden behind a wall at No 158, on the now commercial boulevard Haussmann, the mansion reflects an era when homes were set back from the street for privacy. Enter from the gate at the right end of the wall. It is the start of a long semicircular drive that winds around to the rear of the home. This classic city house has a wide, bow windowed salon facing the street, but these grand homes put their most elaborate faces toward their gardens, which are in back. The Google aerial view shows the only such mansion and garden left in the once elite neighborhood.

**Winter Garden,
Musée Jacquemart-André**

The double staircase in the entry evokes Garnier's opéra house, which was built in the same era. The glass-roofed winter garden is an architectural wonder. Imagine the story of a banking heir who built an idyllic manor, hired a young artist to paint his portrait, fell in love with her, and then married her. It's the stuff of fairy tales. Over their lifetimes, Edouard André and Nélie Jacquemart amassed a museum quality collection of art and furnishings, spanning the Renaissance thru the eighteenth century. Spaced throughout the rooms are works by Botticelli, Canaletto, Rembrandt, Hals, Van Dyck, Fragonard, and Boucher.

**Nelie Jacquemart-
André, *Self Portrait*,
Musée Jacquemart-André**

***Edouard André*, by
Nelie Jacquemart**

There is a pleasant café for lunch in the elegant Louis XV dining room. Use the No 9 Métro to Miromesnil, or the No 28 bus to the stop at Haussmann-Miromesnil.

TWO TOWN HOUSES ON THE PARK

The Parc Monceau, in the 8th Arrondissement, takes credit for being the first high-end gated community in Paris. It was originally laid out in 1779 as a private park with a mélange of English, Chinese, and French garden styles complete with a Pyramid and Roman Columns. Under Napoléon III, half the park was sold off by the aristocratic owners to developers for the building of luxury homes. The other half became a public park, which is only open from sunrise to sunset. Two of the classic town homes are now museums. For both, use the No 30 or 94 bus (Monceau), the No 2 Métro (Monceau) or the No 3 Métro (Villiers).

Entrance, Musée Nissim de Camondo

The Musée Nissim de Commondo is at 63 rue de Monceau. The Comondo families were Sephardic Jews who fled Spain during the Inquisition and founded a bank in Constantinople. Two brothers, Abraham and Nissim, settled in Paris in the 1870s in town houses

Servants' Table, Musée Nissim de Camondo

Dining Room Musée Nissim de Camondo

on the park. Nissim's son Moïse had his town house razed and built a new one in 1914 designed after the Petit Trianon in Versailles. It is lavishly decorated with antique paneling, murals, classic furniture, and Gobelins tapestries. The coming years, however, would bring multiple tragedies to the family. Moïse's son, Nissim, became an Air Force pilot in the First World War and was killed in combat in 1917. When Moïse died in 1935, he left the home and its contents to the City of Paris and named it in honor of Nissim. In the kitchen and scullery, the servants' dinner table is set for dinner. Multiple salons, a library, porcelain, and silver on the tables make the public feel like invited guests. In 1943 and 1944, Moïse's daughter Béatrice, her husband, and children were sent to Auschwitz where they died. The museum stands as a memorial to both the noblest and darkest days of Paris.

At 7 avenue Velasquez, just around the corner, is the Musée Cernuschi. Enrico Cernuschi came to Paris from Italy in 1848. He made

his fortune in banking during the Second Empire, and set out to explore the world. He was smitten with the art and artifacts of Japan and China and built one of Europe's greatest personal collections of Asian art, which he arrayed in the home he built on the edge of the Parc Monceau. He left the home and collection to the City

Musée Cernuschi

Gallery Musée Cernuschi

of Paris. Although the home doesn't have the lived-in look of the previous two, it is still impressive to tour the spacious well-lit rooms that became a museum two years after Cernuschi's death in 1898. Bronzes, Asian carvings, pottery, porcelain, and delicate lacquered pieces are displayed

Chinese Figurine, Musée Cernuschi

in a non-cluttered way that uses the natural light from the immense windows.

The Musée Cognacq-Jay has its roots in the Samaritaine department store, which became the premier place to shop for luxury goods

Jeanne-Madeleine Favier, *Ernest Cognacq*, Musée Cognacq-Jay

Jeanne-Marie Favier, *Marie-Louise Jay*, Musée Cognacq-Jay

when it opened in 1907. Ernest Cognacq and his wife Marie-Louise Jay began their business selling clothes from a street stall and opened their first boutique in 1869. The grand right bank department store they built in 1900 faces the

Pont Neuf. Long appreciated for its combination of Art Déco and Art Nouveau styling and the panoramic views from its rooftop café, the store was closed in 2005 because of structural issues. Rumors have it reopening one day as apartments and office space. Like many of the wealthy of the time, the childless Cognacq-Jays built an extensive collection of 18th and nineteenth century art and furniture which they donated to the City of Paris. The collection had been housed in several locations but in 1990 it

Garden, Musée Cognac Jay

was installed in a 16th century townhouse in the Marais, at No 7 rue Elezvir, near the Place de Vosges. The carved oak paneling from the Cognacq-Jay's original home lines the salons. A small Louvre in itself, the home holds paintings by Rembrandt, Tiepolo, Rubens, Canaletto, Guardi, Boucher, Fragonard, Watteau, and countless other masterworks. The Renaissance

Boudoir, Musée Cognac Jay

Salon, Musée Cognac-Jay

town house has a courtyard and garden and looks like a mini château. Despite the blending of four centuries, it all comes together to impress and delight. Take the No 69 bus to St-Paul or the No 1 or No 7 Métro to the stop of the same name.

The French would say that the art of Gustave Moreau has a certain *je ne sais quoi,* meaning that it's indescribable, but in an intriguing sort of way. Scholars have called him a mystic and a symbolist. The word "*orphisme*", has been used to refer to his "language of light." His dream-state religious and mythical images appear as psychedelic as some of the drug induced art of the 1960s. He could

Musée Gustave Moreau

Gustave Moreau art

Staircase Musée Gustave Moreau

also be credited with anticipating surrealism. He led the secretive life of a loner and rarely exhibited. As a result, his work is still underappreciated today. However, his home reflects the spirit of the artist and his art. Several years before his death in 1898, he began transforming his home into a showplace for his life's work. He designed custom cabinets into the structure that would allow visitors to leaf through portfolios of his smaller works. An elaborate wrought iron circular staircase separates the first and second stories. Large paintings are placed floor to ceiling, and his sculptures appear throughout. His living quarters have been left undisturbed. The residence is a good example of the upper middle class town houses that once filled the neighborhood. The address is 14, rue de la Rochefoucauld. Take the No 12 Métro to the Trinité stop.

A few blocks north of the Musée Gustave Moreau, at 16 rue Chaptal, is the Musée de la Vie Romantique. Although in the same general area as the home of Moreau, this country manor and garden are from a much earlier time, when the neighborhood was a rural suburb called Nouvelle Athènes. The two story manor has a beige exterior with green shutters and is set among rose gardens. It's easy to imagine being in Provence. The museum's name refers to the Romantic Era of art,

Musée de la Vie Romantique

music, and literature during the time that the painter Ary Scheffer lived there from 1830 to 1858. His overly sentimental paintings have not gained him great fame, but his houseguests and salons included George Sand, Sarah Bernhardt, Frédéric Chopin, and Franz Lizst, as well as more renowned painters such as Ingres, Delacroix, and his neighbor, Gustave Moreau. Chopin's études play in the background throughout the sitting rooms. The home and grounds are at their best in the spring and summer when you can enjoy the outdoor café after touring the highly decorated rooms and the art studio. If you plan on lunch between visits to the museums, why not try an excellent

neighborhood bistro? Chez Grenouille at 32 rue Blanche is both authentic and unassuming, just what the local crowd is used to. They respect the classics in the Burgundy tradition. We both had the chicken breast with morille mushrooms.

Salon, Musée de la Vie Romantique

Wines by the glass are inexpensive and won't slow you down (like wines by the bottle).

Victor Hugo was much more than a celebrated writer. He used his fame to champion democratic republicanism—today's form of government in France, as well as social justice and freedom of the press. He suffered for it, at times branded a traitor and living in self-exile. His two most celebrated works, *Les Misérables* and *Notre-Dame de Paris*, known outside of France as *The Hunchback of Notre Dame*, reflected his po-

Victor Hugo

litical and social leanings. One of his residences, the Maison Victor Hugo, in the Place des Vosges is open to the public. This is a wonderful opportunity to go inside

a 17th century town house on the most beautiful square in Paris. His apartment contains several salons and drawing rooms, one of which is decorated and paneled in whimsical Chinese wall carvings that surround a floor to ceiling collection of porcelain plates that belonged to Hugo's

Victor Hugo Apartment

wife, Juliette Drouet. His books

Eugène Delacroix, *Liberty Leading the People*, Louvre

and manuscripts are displayed throughout, along with paintings by Hugo's contemporaries. The views from the rooms onto the Place des Vosges are postcard perfect. The museum is located at No 6 in the Square. No 69 bus stops at Birague and the No 1 or No 7 Métro at St-Paul.

Porcelain Collection, Maison Victor Hugo

Eugène Delacroix (1798-1863) was a rock star in the art world during the period before Impressionism. A leader of the Romantic movement, he brought raw emotion and sometimes blood and gore

Palette of Eugène Delacroix

to vivid heights in his depictions of real and imagined events such as lions attacking and devouring a hunting party. His iconic *Liberty Leading the People* depicts a bare-breasted woman holding the *tricolore* leading a revolutionary charge during the 1830 revolution. The painting can be seen in the Louvre.

This female icon has become the symbol of the Republic. She was the model for the Statue of Liberty, a gift from France to America. In

Delacroix Studio

Musée Delacroix

1857, despite his advanced age and ill health, Delacroix agreed to paint frescoes in a chapel of the Church of St-Sulpice and needed to move close to his work. He located an apartment off the Place Furstenburg, a calm tiny square in the St-Germain-des-Près neighborhood on the left bank. A well-lit studio was set up on an adjoining garden. Just getting to the studio is a treat after entering a secret inner courtyard, traversing the apartment and descending an outside staircase that overlooks another garden hidden to the outside world. Delacroix's best known works are in museums around the world, but smaller, more intricate pieces adorn the walls of his apartment and studio. All in all, the courtyard and garden setting make for a peaceful interlude. Use the No 4 Métro or the No 69 bus to St-Germain.

Honoré de Balzac was broke. Creditors were hounding him day and night. He needed to disappear and find a quiet place to write. He fled to Passy, a village just outside of the city, adopted a pseudonym, and rented a small country house with two exits so he could evade unwelcomed visitors. The next year he succeeded in getting his greatest work published, *The Human Comedy,* a series of stories highlighting human nature with a cast of dozens of colorful characters. He is considered by the French to be a pioneer of the Realism movement. He lived in this house, now called the Maison Balzac, from

Honoré de Balzac

Maison Balzac

1840 to 1847. Today it is surrounded by the 16th Arrondissement of the City of Paris, but its hillside setting still evokes the village life. Inside, dozens of hand engraved lithographic plates used for the pictures in the original volumes show the characters from *The Human Comedy*. The master's writing desk sits in a humble alcove. The garden is open for strolling in Balzac's footsteps. The No 6 Métro stops at

Maison Balzac Interior

Passy, and the 32 bus stops at the rue de Passy. The Maison Balzac is at No 47 rue Raynouard.

The well preserved homes of the rich can appear to have been laid out to display the good taste and the collector's eye of their owners, as if to shout, "We were more than just boring business people who made a lot of money!" We are grateful for their beneficence. On the other hand, the feeling one gets inside the abodes of the artists and writers is of inner struggle culminating in success, often late in life, and ironically, a preference for the Spartan conditions of their youth. Their art, music, and words endure and are enjoyed by generations, while the legacy of the wealthy is more likely to be their acquired wealth.

Musée Baccarat

Crystal Room, Musée Baccarat

Musée Baccarat Ballroom

CHAPTER 6

The Best Museums You Never Heard Of

There are over one hundred fifty museums in Paris. Americans are seldom aware of more than a hand full. Twenty-one of them have been mentioned in previous chapters. Of the rest, some are open by appointment only and not readily accessible. Others are clearly not for everyone: the Museum of Skin Diseases, the Anatomy and Pathology Museum (two headed calves in jars!), the Sewer Museum (right down *in* the sewers!) and the Smoking Museum. This chapter deals with the best of the rest (based solely on my opinion)—either world class in their specialty, one of a kind collections, and those that reveal secrets of Paris to share with friends when you get home. One more has been added that children will love.

A TASTE OF LUXURY

In the mid-1700s, Louis XV granted a royal license to a bishop in Western France to produce glass in the small town of Baccarat. In the early eighteen hundreds, the factory began making leaded crystal stemware which became the rage during the Reign of Louis XVIII. Baccarat crystal chandeliers would adorn homes of the wealthy. Later, color was added to crystal for etched decorative pieces. Perfumes, luxuries in their own right, were sold in handmade crystal bottles. Baccarat crystal became the standard of the Western world. In 2003 the old Baccarat museum, housed in a former company warehouse, was relocated to an elegant mansion that had been built for a countess in 1764. The mansion is large enough to accommodate the company headquarters as well. Baccarat hired Philippe Starck, a superstar designer and architect, to transform the interior on a theme of creative luxury. He did just that. The galleries highlight one of a kind works of art in crystal and special editions from two centuries of coronations, royal weddings, and universal exhibitions. Stunning Baccarat chandeliers adorn the halls. There is no typical museum café. There is the Crystal Room, where elegant lunches and dinners are served. It is expensive. The tables are set with Baccarat crystal. I'll bet the waiters account for the salt shakers before the diners depart. The showroom on the ground floor is anything but an "exit through the gift shop" experience. The *très chic* staff is dressed in little black dresses and suits. Mineral water in Baccarat glasses is served to those browsing the legendary crystal creations. Browsers were all we saw the day of our visit. Outside and across the street is the *Place des Etats-Unis*, or the United States Square. In the center, statues of George Washington and the Marquis de Lafayette watch over children playing. The museum is at No 6, Place des Etats-Unis. The closest stops are Iéna for the No 9

Métro and the 22-30-32-82-63 buses.

Place des Etats-Unis

NEW AND UNCONVENTIONAL

Like most new museums in Paris, the Pinacothèque de Paris generated controversy in 2007 when it opened in a vacant commercial

Pinacothèque de Paris

building on the Place Madeleine. Marc Restellini, the founder, is a noted art historian and the grandson of an artist. He had an idea to convince private collectors to loan him art that may have otherwise never been shown to the public. He also had the personal connections to make it happen. And while Paris has over the years sorted art by genres and periods (Modern to the Pompidou, Impressionism to the Musée d'Orsay), the Pinacothèque displays Picassos and Lichtensteins in between Rembrandts and

Vermeers. A recent exhibit contrasted Giacometti's 20th century stick men to early Etruscan art. Another compared works by Van Gogh to Japanese woodblock prints. The intent seems to be to challenge visitors in a positive way, and it

does exactly that. His unconventional approach has drawn criticism from a jealous art establishment, but the exhibits at the Pinacothèque are always packed. The No 8 Métro stops at the Place de la Madeleine.

Disconnected Comparisons, Pinacothèque de Paris

NO RESPECT!

That's how the Musée du Luxembourg must have once felt—and for good reason. The Luxembourg Gardens that surround the palace of the same name are well known. They hold delights for children: puppet shows, pony rides, high tech playground equipment, and a low tech sailboat pond where toy boats can be rented. Parisians stroll among the extensive gardens that appear to

Jardins du Luxembourg

bloom with every season. The palace itself was completed in 1630 by Marie de Medici, the mother of Louis XIII. Her other children and a succession of royalty lived there until the revolution. Its art collection in-

cluded works by Rubens, Raphaël, Da Vinci, and Rembrandt. In 1750, the collection was the first in France to be opened to the public. In 1815, as the Louvre was expanded, all the art was transferred there, a tough loss. For a while, the Luxembourg Museum showed works of living artists such as

Musée du Luxembourg

Delacroix and Ingres. Then it hosted the first Impressionist exhibit with works by Monet, Sisley, Manet, Renoir, and others. *That* collection was sent to the Musée d'Orsay after it opened in 1977. Since then, the Musée du Luxembourg has found its calling: rotating world class exhibits that celebrate Paris as the capital of the arts and the Renaissance. Shows featuring Botticelli, Titian, and Veronese alternate with those celebrating Cézanne, Matisse, and Vlaminck. The museum's website and Paris

Renoir Exhibit at the Musée du Luxembourg

newspapers highlight current exhibits. Recent shows have featured Cézanne's views of Paris, Chagall's Paris between the wars, and an exhibit honoring Paul Durand-Ruel, the art dealer and collector who discovered and promoted the Impressionists. The museum is in a building that was once the Orangerie of the palace at 19 rue de Vaugirard. Before or after visiting the gardens or museum, lunch at the Restaurant Polidor, 41 rue Monsieur le Prince. It's a one room time machine from 1845 where diners are seated at communal tables while they enjoy traditional French classics at modest prices. Polidor's vintage façade appeared in Woody Allen's *Midnight in Paris*. The streets around the Luxembourg Gardens are well served by public transportation. The No 4 Métro stops at St-Sulpice and the 58-84-89 buses stop next to the gates of the park.

HAVE NO FEAR

On the busy rue Etienne Marcel, near the métro station bearing the same name, stands a medieval tower, the last remaining one in Paris. It was built into a 13th century residence by Jean sans Peur (Fearless John), Duke of Burgundy. It was a time of great violence in France. Jean had his cousin, Louis d'Orléans, King Charles's brother,

Tour Jean sans Peur

assassinated in 1407 setting off a civil war between the Orléans family and the Burgundians. After taking power, Jean renovated his Parisian home, adding the tower in 1411, to be known as the Tour Jean sans Peur. He himself was assassinated in 1419. His grandson lived there until the property was confiscated in 1477. It was used on and off as a residence, shop, and warehouse. In the 1860s when the rue Etienne Marcel was built, the tower became visible from the street. The City of Paris classified it as a historical monument, but left it nearly in ruins. In 1992 it was restored, and in 1999 it was opened as a museum. It celebrates the day-to-day life of the Middle Ages: exhibits on eating and drinking, clothing and fashion, festivals, leisure, and décor, even one on how medieval latrines worked. A recent exhibit was "Love in the Middle Ages." The poster was a bit odd. The vaulted ceiling and the spiral staircase are exceptional and worth a short visit. The tower is at 20, rue Etienne Marcel, near the No 4 Métro stop.

Love in the Middle Ages

IN VINO VERITAS

Paris sits on an ancient plateau of limestone, much of it close to the surface on the steep hillsides near the river. As early as the 13th century, tunnels were dug into the slopes along the Seine across from the Eiffel Tower near present day Passy to mine the soft stone for building. It was transported by boat to central Paris. Over the years, however, the limestone from this area proved to be too porous for construction and the tunnels were abandoned. In the 15th century, an order of monks settled nearby. Their grape arbors lined the hills along the Seine. They discovered the old tunnels and enlarged several of them into vaulted cellars for their wine. After the revolution, the order was dissolved and the cellars and tunnels were abandoned once more. The city grew around them, leaving only a small entrance. They were used in the 1950s by the restaurant in the Eiffel Tower to cellar their extensive wine collection. Then in 1984 the tunnels and cellars were bought

Musée du Vin

History of winemaking, Musée du Vin

Musée du Vin Restaurant

by the *Conseil des Echansons de France*, a society of wine tasters dedicated to preserving the history of wine making. They turned them into the Musée du Vin. The entrance seems out of place in a small square surrounded by upper class apartment buildings. Immediately inside are the vaulted cellars that host daily wine tastings. The ancient tunnels extend four miles into the hills, but only about 1200 feet are used by the museum. The history of wine making is portrayed by life-size wax figures in scenes depicting the wine regions of France, the contributions of Louis Pasteur to wine making, old techniques for making champagne, and craftsmen building wine casks. Collections of Greek and Roman amphorae, sacred chalices, corkscrews, and crystal glasses complete the tour. It was time for lunch! The restaurant's daily menu paired wines with roast pork and lamb stew, just what we needed on an autumn afternoon—all enjoyed beneath the vaulted ceiling. The museum is located at No 5 square Charles Dickens, in the Passy quarter. Use the No 6 Métro or No 72 bus, both at the Passy stop.

WOVEN INTO HISTORY

It's rare to find two structures separated by twelve hundred years as part of the same museum. In this case it's the 3rd century Roman baths and the 15th century Hôtel de Cluny. Romans once ruled Lutetia (Lutèce), the walled city that became Paris. Several vestiges of their presence remain. A Roman amphitheater was uncovered in the 1860s. The thermal baths they built have always been visible as ruins, but have only been seriously studied since the nineteenth century. The baths are comprised of the three traditional rooms: the caldarium (hot), tepidarium (warm), and frigidarium. The Hôtel de Cluny part came much later. Benedictine monks founded the Cluny Abbey in 910 AD in central France as their seat of power in Europe. It was the largest church complex in the world at the time. In the 1300s, the Abbots came from Cluny to Paris to teach at the university. They later had a town house built in the Latin Quarter. In 1843, it became the National Museum of the Middle Ages (Musée National du Moyen Age–Thermes de Cluny). The two structures are only a part of the attraction

Musée du Moyen-Age

here. The rich trove of medieval reliquaries, carvings, stained glass, and weapons would be enough to set this place apart. But there is much more to this institution that makes it a Paris 201 favorite. A set of six tapestries was acquired by the museum in 1882. The coat of arms was from a prominent family from Lyon, France, who had them made in the 15th century. Their size, 15 feet wide by 12 feet long, allows for high detail and intricacy, combining beauty and mystery. The museum guide explains: "The main enigma of this exceptional work of art lies in its meaning. Although the series of tapestries could have been produced to mark the occasion of a major family event, such as

a wedding or betrothal, the fact that the female figures depicted are never the same makes it difficult, if not impossible, to identify such an event and therefore suggests a purely allegorical interpretation." Wait! There must be a story here! That's what Tracy Chevalier thought. Her work

The Lady and the Unicorn

of historical fiction, *The Lady and the Unicorn*, elevated the museum from a favorite of Parisians to a global pilgrimage site for her readers. Her story is as vivid and intricate as the tapestries themselves. It follows the family who commissioned the works and the artisans who created them. There is lust, love, greed, jealousy, and every emotion in between. Each of five works represents one of the five senses: sight, hearing, smell, taste, and touch. The sixth is inscribed "*Mon seul désir*" ("My only desire."), interpreted by some as the sixth sense, either the intellect or the heart—or maybe the struggle between the two.

The tapestries are hung in a special room with indirect light to prevent damage. Reading the book before seeing the tapestries will let your mind's eye prepare for the real thing. In the Roman ruins, the frigidarium is the only complete room still intact. In 1836, it was modified to house Roman artifacts unearthed around Paris. It also holds another secret. Across the facade of the Notre-Dame Cathedral stand the statues of the twenty-eight kings of Judah. During the French Revolution, thinking that they were kings of France, angry mobs decapitated them. The statues were later restored with new heads under the reign of Napoléon. Then in 1977, twenty-one of the original heads were unearthed in a garden, perhaps buried there during the rioting by a sympathetic Parisian. The heads are displayed in the frigidarium, looking out stoically on visitors, still showing the scars from the beating they took. There is still one headless statue on the front of Notre-Dame, but this one, St-Denis, is

Kings of Judah Notre-Dame

Heads from Notre-Dame in the Musée du Moyen-Age

St-Denis, at Notre-Dame

holding his head in his hands. The first bishop of Paris, and the patron Saint of France, is said to have been beheaded, by the Romans no less,

in 250 AD. According to legend, St-Denis then picked up his head and walked up to what is now called Montmartre, or the hill of the martyr. The ruins of the thermal baths are visible at the corner of the boulevard St-Germain and the boulevard St-Michel. The Hôtel de Cluny is set behind them at the Place Paul Painlevé. The métro stops are Cluny-La

Thermal Bath Ruins

Sorbonne and St-Michel. It is well served by buses: 21-27-38-63-86-87, or by the No 10 Métro to the Cluny-La Sorbonne stop.

ASIAN FUSION

Whenever possible, we like to combine a museum visit with lunch. In the case of the Musée Guimet, the lunch is part of the experience. France's National Museum of Asian Arts was named for the industrialist Emile Guimet, who donated his art collection. Its original theme when it opened in 1889 was the history of religions. Today, its 45,000 sculptures, paintings, and art objects span 3000 years of history. They are organized geographically: India, China, Central Asia, Nepal-Tibet, Pakistan-Afghanistan, Southeast Asia, Korea, and Japan. The interior of the classic building has been completely restructured. Its stark white curves evoke Frank Lloyd Wright's Guggenheim design. The four spacious floors totaling 50,000 square feet never feel crowded. The Buddhas seem to chant in every key as you walk among them. My "smart" camera kept telling me that the subject of the photo blinked. I finally realized that it was caused by the Buddha's serene pose with closed eyes. A second building holds the "Buddhist pantheon", where works are set in a peaceful bamboo garden. The restaurant on the lower level, "Les Porcelaines", serves jasmine tea with Asian themed choices like dim sum, sesame noodles, sea bass with ginger, and Thai style salmon. We often go back just for lunch! The museum is located at No 6 Place

Musée Guimet

Musée Guimet Gallery

Les Porcelaines, Musée Guimet

Musée Guimet Mask

Musée Bourdelle

d'Iéna. Métro stops are Iéna for the No 9 and Boissière for the No 6, and the 82 bus stops near the front of the building.

THINKING BIG

Antoine Bourdelle was a student of and later an assistant to Auguste Rodin. He is considered to be a "monumental" sculptor, referring to his outsized statues, reliefs, and equestrians. His atelier, apartment, and sculpture gardens comprise the Musée Bourdelle,

Musée Bourdelle Interior

Antoine Bourdelle, Gustave Eiffel

at 18 rue Antoine Bourdelle, in a quiet corner of Montparnasse. The sculptor worked and lived there from 1884 until his death in 1929. The cavernous brick buildings have a pantheon-like presence, with large-scale works on display. His sculptures around Paris include the portal of the Musée Grévin, the monument to the Polish poet Adam Mickiewicz near the Pont de l'Alma, the bronze bust of Gustave

Eiffel at the famous tower, and the marble friezes on the exterior of the Théâtre des Champs-Elysées. Other works decorate museums around the world. The sheer size of the museum complex makes it hard to believe that it stays so hidden and unknown. The closest métro and bus stops are the ones that stop at the Gare Montparnasse railroad station.

SENSUAL AND SPIRITUAL

Known for his sense of naturalism and realism, Jean-Jacques Henner walked a line between the Impressionists and the Romantics around the close of the nineteenth century. The Musée National Jean-Jacques Henner displays in art the chronological life history of the artist. It begins with his youth in Alsace, then to Rome where he won the Prix de Rome for his emotional rendering of *Adam and Eve Finding the Body of Abel*, then to his prize at the Paris Exposition of 1900. His sensual nudes are not quite Rubenesque but still robust, perhaps reflecting his Alsacian heritage. Graphic

Musée National, Jean-Jacques Henner

portrayals of the passion and death of Christ are profoundly spiritual. Hazy, shadowy borders surround his subjects, blurring the lines between them and the background. His works also adorn the Musée d'Orsay and the National Gallery in Washington, DC. The four story mansion housing his museum sits at 42 avenue de Villiers. It was originally the home of Guillaume Dubufe, an artist contemporary of Henner. It was purchased by Henner's heirs and opened to

Jean-Jacques Henner, *Adam and Eve finding the Body of Abel*

the public in 1924, almost twenty years after his death. The ground floor displays portraits of himself, his wife, and family. The two floors above reflect his time in Rome and Paris. The top floor studio is awash in light and holds many of his sketches and preparatory works. On the cold day of our visit we stopped first for lunch at Le

Studio, Musée Henner

Petit Villiers (Chez Fred) at 75 avenue de Villiers, right across from the Villiers stop of the No 3 Métro. Salads, duck confit, lamb chops, soups, and classic desserts grace the unbelievably low fixed priced menu.

A TIME MACHINE

As the end of the nineteenth century approached, continued modernization put at risk some of the city's most beautiful and historic

Furniture, Musée des Arts Décoratifs

residences that happened to find themselves in the way of new construction. A group of craftsmen, industrialists, and collectors were determined to save the decorative arts of the past. They arranged for entire rooms to be disassembled and reinstalled along with their furniture and *objets d'art* in a recently restored wing of the Louvre that was opened as a separate museum. The Musée des Arts Décoratifs opened in 1904 in the Marsan Pavillon at 107 rue de Rivoli. It is often overlooked or passed by assuming that it is part of the Louvre itself. Its collection is organized by period, with rooms and collections starting with the Middle Ages

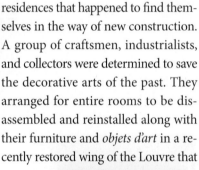

Medieval Room

Carrousel du Louvre

followed by the Renaissance, then by century from the 17th through the nineteenth. It continues with 20th century movements in design: Art Nouveau, Art Déco, Modern, and Contemporary. Other areas are devoted to design in glass, jewelry, wallpaper, and toys. An impressive non sequitur is the Dubuffet Gallery, the only one devoted to Jean Dubuffet, the 20th century artist who did not like museums. The collection of paintings, sculptures, and works on paper was donated by the artist in 1967 because of his

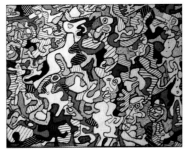

Dubuffet Gallery at the Musée des Arts Décoratifs

friendship with the head curator of the museum. The museum restaurant, the Saut du Loup, extends out to the lawns of the Carrousel du Louvre, one of the most beautiful alfresco settings in Paris. Its daily lunch menu as well as its décor is both simple and elegant.

SUB SAHARA

In 1668, Olfert Dapper, a Dutch humanist, published *A Description of Africa*. It became the definitive text for generations of Africanists. A foundation was set up in 1983 to raise the profile of sub Saharan Africa's artistic heritage. The Musée Dapper was established in 2000. We came across the museum when we were walking down the avenue Victor Hugo and saw a sign pointing down the quiet rue Paul Valéry. We returned the next day to find a well-organized collection of art and cultural artifacts from sub Sahara Africa displayed in softly lit, earth toned galleries. A suspended walkway from the entrance looks down on the restaurant

Musée Dapper Gift Shop

and boutique on the floor below. The ground floor and first floor hold sculptures, tools, crafts, and religious objects. A recent photo exhibit showed the royal thrones of tribal kings. Another show highlighted the influence of African sculpture on the young Picasso. A 190 seat

Musée Dapper Masks

auditorium has hosted plays, music, dance, children's programs, and films relating to the art and culture of Africa and its diaspora. The restaurant is pleasant and the boutique has great African inspired jewelry. The No 1 Métro stop at Charles De Gaulle-Etoile or the 82 bus to Victor Hugo are the closest points to the museum.

A MAGIC MOMENT

On each visit to Paris with our grandchildren, we take them to the Musée de la Magie, or Magic Museum. It's open Wednesday, Saturday, and Sunday afternoons, all "no school" days in Paris. It is housed in 16th century caves (cellars) in the ancient Marais district. The docents who run it are lovers of magic, putting on continuous shows that amaze and amuse children and their parents and grandparents. Fortune telling machines, scary swamis, props from travelling shows,

Musée de Magie

human size boxes for sawing people in half or making them disappear, and a large collection of automated carnival games (some only slightly risqué) will keep the kids and adults entertained for an afternoon. The museum shop sells inexpensive magic tricks and gags. The staff will patiently teach children how to use them so they can put on their own magic shows when they get home. The address is 11 rue St-Paul. St-Paul is the No 1 Métro stop as well as the No 69 bus stop.

SIX HUNDRED YEARS AGO AT THE END OF THE LINE

Not quite a museum in the traditional sense, but better! A 14th century castle at a métro stop. The No 1 Métro was the first to be built. It runs east-west across Paris. It originally connected two of the old gates into the city, the porte Maillot on the west and the porte de Vincennes on the east. It was extended over time and now runs from La Défense, the 20th century commercial center west of Paris, to the Château de Vincennes, 600 years away by métro (twenty minutes or so from the Place de la Concorde).

When it dawned on King Charles V back in the 1300s that the expanding city limits of Paris were making it more difficult to escape the Louvre from angry mobs in times of unrest, he began constructing a fortified town for his family far from the city (but not so far today). Charles was the first of many kings to despise living in Paris, and his château has been referred to as the medieval Versailles.

Parc Floral

It's easy to be stunned while emerging from the Château de Vincennes Métro exit and seeing the outer walls, moat, drawbridge and tower of a 14th century castle. The tower, called the "dungeon", was added as it expanded into a residence. It has its own moat and drawbridge. Today, inside the walls can be found improvements by just about every ruler since, including the addition of a handsome chapel. Because of its similarity, I asked a guide if it was based on the design of the Sainte-Chapelle in Paris, built by Louis IX (St-Louis). He said the opposite was true, that Louis built the chapel here first. Nobody has lived in the château since the revolution, although the Marquis de Sade was imprisoned there in the years leading up to it. The modern parc floral de Paris which opened in 1998 starts behind the château in the bois de Vincennes, the old royal hunting grounds. It features flower shows, lakes, and paths for strolling. The castle and park are great for letting children run around until they are tired. Across the street from the castle gate in this carefree town is a pleasant brasserie, Le Drapeau, where locals and castle visitors go to lunch.

Château de Víncennes Dungeon

La Chapelle, Château de Víncennes

View from
Palais de
Chaillot

CHAPTER 7

Villages in the City and the Railway that Connected Them

ew York has been called a city of neighborhoods. Paris is literally a city of villages that once existed outside the perimeter of the city walls. As the walls came down and the city expanded, these villages were absorbed into the new city limits. The last such expansion occurred in 1860, when Baron Haussmann, directed by Napoléon III to remake Paris, annexed sixteen surrounding villages. Paris expanded from twelve to twenty arrondissements, the configuration that exists today. The expansion probably didn't surprise anyone at the time. The city limits were marked by the Farmers-General tax wall. It was simply a barrier designed to collect taxes on materials entering the city. New fortifications were constructed in the 1840s, the Thiers wall, which circled the city but from outside the city limits. The sixteen villages lay in the land between the two concentric walls. Today's *Périphérique*, the highway around Paris, runs along the site of the old Thiers wall.

The villages had town halls, squares, and churches. A few had their own château or remnants of royal residences. Several had their own railway station on the Petite Ceinture, a "little beltway" that circled the city, connecting the big rail stations. Two and three centuries of architecture are mixed on the narrow streets. Most of these villages are still middle or working class today, but are showing signs of creeping gentrification as Parisian yuppies restore vintage apartments and rediscover village life. The only really famous one is Montmartre. Its town square, the Place du Tertre, has evolved into a confluence of clichés: touristy restaurants, souvenir art probably made elsewhere, and shoulder-to-shoulder crowds. Just two of the villages, Passy and Auteuil, could be considered affluent, but they all give off the same aura of satisfied villagers who wouldn't ever want to live "in the city." Despite having been sewn into the fabric of Paris,

Place du Tertre

some of these villages can come alive again if you know where to look.

GRENELLE

Grenelle was the first village we discovered. We frequently take the No 8 Métro to the rue du Commerce, two stops south of Ecole Militaire. The street has several clothing stores for children and adults, not designer boutiques but family stores with family prices. The rue du Commerce has all the other necessities covered too: butchers, bakeries, fish, and vegetable markets. Over time we discovered that it was a self-contained village before 1860. In 1824, about 200 acres were subdivided from the village of Vaugirard by several optimistic businessmen, hence the names like rue du Commerce and square des Entrepreneurs. The new village was named Grenelle. Léonard Violet, one of the founders, built a château near the center.

At the Commerce Métro stop, exit for the rue du Commerce. It opens at the edge of a rectangular park with a gazebo in the center. Walk around the perimeter to the other end of the park. There stands

Grenelle town hall

the former town hall, still inscribed with "*Liberté Egalité Fraternité*", the motto of France. It does not appear to be completely abandoned, but it's not obvious what it's used for today. Go back to the rue du Commerce and walk in the direction of the church.

Rue du Commerce and St-Jean Baptiste

Construction of the church of St-Jean Baptiste was started immediately after the subdivision was created in 1824. It has been expanded several times. Facing the front of the church, turn right on the rue des Entrepreneurs. Walk to the Place Violet, which will be on the left. A modern firehouse stands in front of the Château Violet. I always walk through the center doorway of the firehouse—no one has ever stopped me—to see the stone façade. A gate at the right front of the

Château Violet

firehouse leads to a park on the former grounds of the château. The back of the château is not as imposing as the front. Violet lost the château in 1827 to creditors after living in it for only a few years. After the annexation of Grenelle, the City of Paris took over the château and built the fire station in front of it. The residence is now used for administration and training. At the back of the park, exit and

Square behind Eglise St-Jean Baptiste

turn left on the rue de l'Eglise, which heads back to the church. A narrow lane, the Impasse de l'Eglise, contains a row of small houses that

Impasse de l'Eglise

doubled as workshops for tradesmen. The one sign left hanging is for a cabinet and furniture maker. Ahead, the square in back of the church is a particularly pleasant setting with trees and a fountain. Walk around the church and back toward the métro stop. Continue up the rue du Commerce and check out the many stores that keep the villagers self-sufficient. At number 51 is the Café du Commerce, one of the nicest neighborhood restaurants in all of Paris. It's one of a kind; three stories in an open balconied hall and a changing menu of classic dishes. Our granddaughters love the steak frites. The rue du Commerce continues with wider sidewalks that make it almost pedestrian only. At number 27, cross the street and look up at the old sign and glass panels

Café du Commerce Interior

for the "La Grande Crèmerie de Grenelle", where the locals as well as the city folk would come to get their milk, butter, and cream. There is now a boutique in the space. It's a short walk back to the Ecole Mili-

27 rue de Commerce

taire as this street turns into the avenue de la Motte-Picquet. The rue du Commerce has great shopping, a wonderful restaurant, plenty of village ambience, and it's close to our apartment. When we take visitors there, they all say the same thing, "I could live here!"

BATIGNOLES

In 1870, a painting by Henri Fantin-Latour entitled *Un Atelier aux Batignoles* was exhibited at the Paris Salon. It now hangs in the Musée d'Orsay. The work depicts a group of artists considered to be avant-garde at the time: the Impressionists, Edouard Manet, Auguste Renoir, Claude Monet, and Frédéric Bazille, sculptor Zacharie Astruc, writer Emile Zola, and a few others less notable. Everyone is dressed up and posed. Manet is in the process of painting Astruc while others look on. The group became known as the *Ecole des Batignoles* from the vil-

Henri Fantin-Latour, *Un Atelier aux Batignoles*, Musée d'Orsay

lage they lived and worked in at the time. The neighborhood was near the Gare St-Lazare, whose trains travelled north to the country villages of Normandy where the Impressionists painted on weekends. Both the station and the town figure in many of their works. Batignoles started as a small hamlet where well-off Parisians kept their second homes. Like most of the other villages around Paris, it is on an elevated plain that slopes down toward the Seine and the central city. The high ground was perfect for the windmills that once all but circled Paris.

The name Batignoles is derived from a word meaning country house. It was a royal hunting ground, and then was claimed by farmers after the revolution and the village began to take shape. The village grew from 6,000 inhabitants in 1830 to 65,000 in 1860, partly fueled by an exodus of Parisians during the revolution of 1848.

To approach the village, take the 66 bus from the Place de l'Opéra to the stop Mairie du XVIIe (the town hall of the 17th Arrondissement). On the way to this stop, the bus passes the Gare Saint-Lazare

Edouard Manet, *The Railway*, National Gallery of Art, Washington DC

and the Place de l'Europe, which overlooks the railyard. Manet's enigmatic painting of a mother and child, *The Railway*, is the view from the Place de l'Europe. Across from the bus stop on rue des Batignoles is the Place Baret, a small leafy square where markets are sometime set up on weekends. An eight foot tall, dark green cast iron monolith stands on the square, a Wallace fountain. An Englishman living in Paris, Sir Richard Wallace, funded the building of public fountains to alleviate the scarcity of drinking water in the 1870s after the Franco-Prussian War. Water streams downward from a dome supported by four robed female statues. The fountains operate only from March 15 to November 15 to avoid the risk of freezing. Originally there were tin cups on chains attached to them, but they were later deemed unhygienic and removed in the 1950s. Today, sixty-seven of the large fountains are scattered around the city, many of them like this one, in the squares of the old villages. Robert Doisneau's iconic 1946 photo of children climbing the fountain in the Place St-Sulpice shows how they were an integral part of the neighborhoods.

Wallace Fountain, Place Baret

Robert Doisneau, Wallace Fountain, Place St-Sulpice 1946, Getty Images

St-Marie des Batignoles

Walk toward the church at the end of the street. Further down the rue des Batignoles are examples of how these villages manage to survive modernization. There is no preservation society for shops and cafés. It's just that the rents are low and the locals are happy to continue to shop in their neighborhood. On the side streets of these villages some all-but-lost *métiers* continue to apply their craft. Signs read: *serrurier* (locksmith), *ébeniste* (furniture maker), *mercier* (haberdasher), *menuisier* (carpenter), *luthier* (stringed instrument maker), *tapissier* (upholsterer), and *horlogers* (watchmaker). In some other "untouched" neighborhoods where rapid gentrification takes place, rising rents kill off these shops like the plague, as name brand boutiques invade.

Altar, St-Marie de Batignoles

The entrance to the square is filled by the Greek columned church. St-Marie de Batignoles was built in 1826 in the center of the village. Its name is based on the legend of a worker finding a statue of the Virgin Mary during excavations. The exterior is plain, but the interior is a combination of baroque and Roman influence. Above and behind the altar is a statue of the virgin and child suspended in a sky blue grotto.

Photographie

Tapissier

Ebénisterie-Menuiserie

Village Scene

Chez Felixio

The wide, tree-covered promenade that circles the church comes alive on weekends. Cafés and restaurants on the square fill with older couples and young families who are attracted to living here by the low real estate prices and rents. We ate lunch at Chez Felixio on the square near the rear of the church where another Wallace fountain stands guard. At our table on the outdoor terrace we each enjoyed a *salade de chèvre chaud*, a warm goat cheese topped salad with the standard vinaigrette dressing. Our table overlooked the entrance to the parc des Batignoles, one of the lesser known works of Jean-Charles Alphand,

who designed the gardens in the bois de Vincennes, the bois de Boulogne, and the parc Montsouris. Landscaped green spaces, towering trees, lakes with swans and ducks make one almost forget about city life but the sounds of trains from

Parc des Batignoles

the Gare Saint-Lazare bring back reality. To the right at the back of the park is a bridge over the rail lines with a small station perched at one end, the Gare du Pont Cardinet. It was the Batignoles station for the

Petite Ceinture that once circled Paris. Today it serves the suburban RER rail line. Back at the entrance to the park by the square is the stop for the No 66 bus that runs back to the Opéra.

Gare du pont Cardinet

VAUGIRARD

Even after the small village of Grenelle was partitioned in 1824, the larger town of Vaugirard still occupied the rest of what became the 15th Arrondissement in 1860. In the 13th century, the land was cultivated by Benedictine monks. The name comes from the word *val* (valley) and *Girard* the first name of the Abbot of St-Germain-des-Prés. The two words became Vaugirard. The town suffered from pillaging during the Hundred Years' War (1337-1453) and had a bout with the black plague, but other than that, it was a blissful, pastoral village. The main street, the rue de Vaugirard, follows an ancient Roman road. It is the longest street in Paris, extending all the way to the Luxembourg Gardens. Up until the-mid-Nineteenth Century, the area was still a place for country houses. Stone quarries, vineyards, and turnip farms were spread throughout the area. The annexation of the village by the City of Paris in 1860 was not at all welcomed by the citizens of Vaugirard. They believed they were entirely self-sufficient and nothing good could come of it. They were right! Their town hall was torn down to build the new *mairie* for the 15th Arrondissement. Where vineyards once stood, an immense slaughterhouse was built in 1894 to supply Paris with meat. A horse market was added in 1904. The horse is still a prominent symbol in the neighborhoods of Vaugirard. The slaughterhouses were closed in 1975 and replaced by modern grassy parks. One can still find a vineyard, small detached houses with a rural look, an old elevated section of the Petite Ceinture that is becoming the newest high line of Paris, and an iconic artist colony, *La Ruche (*the Beehive*)*, where Chagall, Léger, and Soutine lived when they were poor.

Vaugirard is unlike the other villages. It's spread over a much larger area. There is no one single town center. It's worth spending a day there. Bringing a street map would be helpful. Because of the distances, the walking tour is split into two parts, although it's possible to do them both in one day.

The first part starts at the park on the site of the old slaughterhouse and horse market. Take the No 95 bus to the Brancion stop. Walk back in the direction the bus came from on the rue Brancion. A bridge spans the abandoned tracks of the Petite Ceinture. There were actually two stations in Vaugirard, one for passengers, still standing, and one, since destroyed, at the slaughterhouse for delivering livestock. Continue down the rue Brancion, the wrought iron and tile covered shelters of the horse

Vaugirard Book Market

market stand quietly to the left. On weekends they are home to a used and vintage book market. I was there on a Thursday and a vintage vinyl album and postcard market attracted a crowd. On the

Gate to Horse Market

corner of the rue Briancion and rue des Morillons is the stone gate to the former horse market, with a horse's head over the portico. Just inside is another Wallace fountain, a sign of a working class neighborhood. Across the street is a café, the *Cent Kilos.* The gate and the café are related. *Cent kilos,* or 100 kilograms, about 220 pounds, was the weight that the butchers were supposed to be able to lift in the slaughter house. Inside the horse market is a statue of a butcher hoisting his 100 kilos. A word here about horsemeat in Paris. After the French Revolution, horses owned by aristocrats were butchered for their meat by hungry commoners. During Napoléon's war campaigns, army surgeons advised starving troops to eat the meat of horses fallen in battle.

Wallace Fountain, Vaugirard

Cent Kilos

Then during the 1870 siege of Paris and the near famine conditions, the locals regained their taste for horsemeat. There are still a dozen horse butchers (*boucheries chevalines*) in Paris, mostly in working class neighborhoods, and half as many restaurants that serve it. Eating horsemeat is still socially acceptable in France. Even if it is not acceptable to Americans, it's a part of the history of Vaugirard.

Walk down the rue des Morillons to the grand entrance to the slaughterhouses, marked by two bronze bulls on pedestals. A clock tower (belfry) sits in the distance on a small lake. The slaughterhouses and horse market were torn down in 1974. A magnificent park was built and named after George Brassens, a singer songwriter who lived

Slaughterhouse Entrance

Bell Tower, Parc Georges Brassens

Parc Georges Brassens

in the neighborhood. This eighteen-acre piece of heaven is in sharp but pleasant contrast to what went on here for almost 100 years. In it there are puppet shows for children, walking trails, wild flowers, ponds with ducks and swans, honey producing beehives, and a theater. Lonely

donkeys await children to ride them. The park holds the last of the Vaugirard vineyards, planted in Pinot Noir grapes. Each year, wine is bottled from the vineyard and sold at the town hall. Take the time to experience all of the park.

Vaugirard Vineyard

Exit the park through the same main entrance. Across the street is a small square, the Place Jacques Marette. A good restaurant, Arthur et Juliette, is convenient for lunch. Continue along the rue des Morillons. The building at the end of the park is the lost and found department of the City of Paris. It's called the department of *objets trouvés* (found objects). Inside is a small muse-um that displays the incredible items

Lost and Found Museum

found but unclaimed: a wooden leg, several skulls, and the more mundane items left in taxis.

At the corner of the rue de Dantzig, there is a modern version of a half-timbered building. Turn left and walk up the hill toward the ta-bac-Café Dantzig. To the left is a passage. At the beginning is a gated courtyard. Inside is an octagonal building. In 1900, Alfred Boucher, a philanthropist and art patron, bought a brick building from the closed Paris Universal Exhibition and had it moved to a vacant lot where it

now sits. He called it *La Ruche*—the beehive. He leased spaces for a pittance to the poorest of the poor artists. Chagall, Poutine, Léger, Zadkine, Modigliani, and Matisse lived there before they could af-ford to move to Montparnasse. Chagall even left some paintings

La Ruche

there that were supposedly burned for firewood. Later, moderns such as Bernard Buffet used La Ruche during his starving artist days. The building was listed for sale in the 1960s by the heirs of the founder. The City of Paris, supported by funding from Americans, saved La Ruche, which, now modernized with creature comforts like indoor plumbing, still houses up-and-coming artists selected by competition. There is a No 89 bus stop on the corner of the rue de Dantzig and the rue des Morillons that goes back to central Paris.

The second half of the Vaugirard tour begins by taking the No 80 bus (which stops at the Ecole Militaire) to the porte de Versailles, the end of the line. It is the site of a large exhibition and sports complex. This is just inside the current city limits, but before 1860 it was still the village of Vaugirard. In recent years, a tram line has been built along the periphery of Paris that closely follows the old Petite Ceinture. Cross over the tram tracks and turn right. At the corner of the rue de Vaugirard is a restaurant, Chez

Le Tram

Clément. The dozens of copper saucepans hanging on the corner are a

Chez Clément

trademark of this chain. Turn left onto Vaugirard and walk toward a rail overpass. Above it is the old Gare de Vaugirard of the Petite Ceinture. Take the stairs to the level of the tracks. The station has three stories, from street level to the tracks. Although abandoned, this section of the tracks now has a new life as a high line with walking trails where the tracks once were. There are also plans in place to renovate the orphaned station. On the other side of the tracks along the right of way, tennis courts have been built, a common use for the land along the old railway.

Gare de Vaugirard

Now walk to the No 80 bus stop at the corner of Vaugirard—Croix-Nivert—and take it to the Cambronne-Vaugirard stop.

Vaugirard Horse Butcher

The rue Cambronne starts here on the left. What is remarkable about it is the village-within-a-village feel that intensifies as you approach the rue Lecourbe. Near the corner on the left is one of Paris' remaining *boucheries chevalines*. A noble horsehead sculpture, haloed in neon, sets it apart from the neighboring charcuterie, *poissonnerie*, and other food markets. It is unashamed of its presence. After all this is Vaugirard. Who knows if the *boucherie chevaline* will have another generation of customers? Turn right on rue Lecourbe. At No 77 is a genuine and humble Auvergne restaurant, Le Café Chastel. The Auvergnats came to Paris from central France in the 1860's, first selling firewood, coal, and wine, and later opening some of the best neighborhood restaurants, which were called Bougnats. On our first visit, the owner, or *patron,* was behind

Horse Head

the bar toasting his lunchtime worker friends with Pastis. Any one of them looked as though he could hoist 100 kilos. We have enjoyed their salads as well as the duck, beef, veal and chicken. Vaugirard is still for the villagers, many of them from the working class of its heritage.

Café Chastel

It is a given that restaurants will serve good, hearty food at affordable prices.

After lunch, walk back to the rue de Vaugirard and turn right. Several blocks away on the right is the rue Gerbert and the church of St-Lambert de Vaugirard. It was built in 1853 in the Neo Romanesque style, on the site of the original church that dated back to the 14th century. The old church supposedly contained the relics of St-Lambert, Bishop of Maastricht.

Vaugirard has been through a lot. It will never pastoral again. Nor will it ever be industrialized again. While it seems to be content with the working class status, its low rents and property prices make it ripe for gentrification.

The No 80 bus stops at the corner of Cambronne and Vaugirard and heads back to central Paris.

St-Lambert de Vaugirard

BERCY

The area that became the village of Bercy has a long history. The oldest evidence of human habitation around Paris, a dugout canoe, tools and pottery, dating back 4000 years, were discovered there in 1992. The canoe can be seen in the Musée Carnavalet. The name Bercy dates to the twelfth century. A village grew around the Château de

Drawing of the Château de Bercy, Louvre

Bercy built in the 1600s. The tax walls constructed around the City of Paris in the 1780s kept the village out of the city, but put it on the map for other reasons. While duty-free wine was an attraction at the guingettes in all of the villages outside the tax walls, in Bercy, it was big business. A port on the Seine near today's Gare de Lyon, Bercy was the destination for

wine from Burgundy and wood from the Morvan region. Stone warehouses or *chais* built for storing wine lined the quays. Parisians flocked there for the double benefit of duty free *and* wholesale prices. The 1860 annexation changed all that. Bercy lost its duty-free status and became just another port on the Seine. In the 1980s much of the

Bercy Wine Warehouses

area was redeveloped. The finance ministry, a sports arena, and a new train station were built; but the quarter of the wine warehouses was restored and ironically renamed Bercy Village, its status before 1860. Bercy is best reached by the No 24 bus that runs from the Place de la Concorde along the right bank and returns along the left bank. Exit at the Dijon-Lachambeaudie stop. The return stop is just across the street on the rue de Bercy. There are lots of restaurants a few minutes away

Cartouche Café

when you get to old Bercy Village, but take special note of the Cartouche Café near the return stop. It has a creative, reasonable menu and is filled each day by locals. The village church is just ahead. The fact that it sits on an island surrounded by traffic is a reminder that parts of Bercy have been extensively redeveloped. It's still called the Place Lachambeaudie despite having been encroached upon by the widening of the streets around it. Watch for traffic and cross over to the church. Notre-Dame de la Nativité de Bercy was finished in 1826 on the site of several previous versions. It has had a rather unlucky history. It was burned during the Paris Commune of 1870, the only church in the city to suffer that fate. The rebuilding did not go well, and it wasn't until the end of the century that it was completed. In 1910 it was inundated by the historic floods

Notre-Dame de la Nativité de Bercy

that swept Paris. It was bombed in 1944 in an allied attack on the Bercy rail yard. Another fire occurred in 1982 and a remodeling took place in 1985. After suffering in the Commune, the bishop gave the church several 17th and 18th century paintings which survived and are on display. These, and a modern sculpture of the *Bon*

Le Bon Larron

Larron (the penitent theif) on a crucifix, make a short visit worthwhile. Leave the front of the church and continue back on the rue de Dijon which turns into the rue Joseph Kessel. Turn left at the beginning of the parc de Bercy on the rue d'Ambroisie. The parc was built in 1995 on land once used by wine merchants to store their vintages. The redevelopment of the quarter included many new apartment blocks which are populated by young families. At the end of the street enter the cour

Bercy Village

Pavillons de Bercy

St-Emilion. (Note the street names based on the famous wines of France.) Rows of beige stone warehouses face each other along a lively pedestrian-only street. Nearly all of them are trendy gourmet shops and terraced restaurants that quickly fill at lunchtime, particularly in mild weather. In the evenings, another old warehouse complex behind the cour St-Emilion hosts concerts, art shows, and plays.

CHARONNE (PAVILLON DE L'ERMITAGE)

What draws the curious to Charonne is a beautiful Regency era pavillon in a small park, but that is only part of the attraction in what may be the last authentic village in Paris. To approach the village take the No 3 Métro in the direction of Galliéni to the porte de Bagnolet. The No 5 exit opens on the Place Edith Piaf, named for the "Little Sparrow" who was born nearby in 1915. Her life's story in the movie *La Vie en Rose* recounts her growing up in the squalor of nearby Belleville. Her statue in the otherwise nondescript square was erected in 2003 on the fortieth anniversary of her

Place Edith Piaf

death. The life-size work emphasizes how tiny she was. A Wallace fountain in the small triangular space evokes its working class past. Across from the Place Edith Piaf there is an industrial looking complex where maintenance is done on commuter rail cars. Alongside is the rue du Capitaine Ferber. At the bottom of the street on the corner is Le Bistro du Parisien, one of the most authentic neighborhood

Le Bistro Parisien

restaurants we have found. The convivial atmosphere here is contagious. Area workers on their lunch break enjoy the plat du jour while couples of a "certain age" linger over three course lunches. On our last visit we both started with the duck terrine with figs, then the grilled lamb with lentils for my wife and roasted duck breast in wine sauce and roasted potatoes for me. We shared a light Bordeaux. It was simple home cooking that would be seen as elegant and probably expensive in the U.S.

After lunch, we turned left on the rue Pelleport. At the end of the short street, across the rue de Bagnolet, is the Pavillon de l'Hermitage, just inside the gates to a park. It is all that remains of the Château de Bagnolet which sat at the edge of the village of Charrone. The original

Château de Charonne was built around 1600 in the countryside east of the old city walls amid gypsum mines, farms, and vineyards. It changed hands several times among royalty. In 1719, Philippe of Orleans, the Regent of France during Louis XV's

Pavillon de l'Hermitage

childhood, bought the estate for his wife, the Duchess of Orleans. They enlarged the 200 acres of gardens and rebuilt the château in the Regency style. The name was changed to the Château de Bagnolet. It was common at the time to construct totally useless, whimsical outbuildings called "follies" in the parks of châteaux. For example, Versailles has a tiny farm where the queen could play milkmaid. Others had miniature Roman temples to Diana, the goddess of the hunt. Three "follies" were added to the grounds. All but one, the Pavillon de l'Hermitage, was destroyed in the 1800s and the land subdivided. The building was known as the "palace of the hermits" because of the religious paintings on interior panels depicting the lives of the hermit-saints of the desert. Some were graphic enough to be deemed indecent at the time, and the naked hermits have since been clothed in the paintings. The pavilion was used strictly as a summer retreat for salons and games. One can imagine royal families strolling in the surrounding park. While the exterior is in the Regency style,

Interior, Pavillon de l'Hermitage

interior décor is more in the Rococo manner. Inside, there are no furnishings, but a photography exhibit shows the area's transformation over the last 150 years.

On the adjacent corner sits the restaurant Le Papillon (The Butterfly), a perfect companion to the pavillon and another ideal place to stop for lunch. The dining room is not large but still spacious. Modern sculpture adorns the bright windowed alcoves. As in most neighborhoods where twenty and thirty-something's hang out, "le brunch" is all the rage these days on weekends, and the Papillon was serving it to singles and young families. The daily menu takes old standards and makes them modern without derailing them. On the day my son and I were there I had a chef's

Le Papillon

salad with foie gras on toast, smoked duck, haricots verts, lettuce, and tomatoes. My son had scallops en brochette with steamed carrots and broccoli with a hint of curry. Lunch was not expensive. Our expectations were exceeded.

After lunch, we began our walk down the rue de Bagnolet from the high ground of the chateau. It appears that the street has been widened

Rue de Bagnolet, Charonne

and the slope has been changed from what was once a steep narrow lane. This is evidenced by unusual double staircases on the front of two homes on the left and the retaining wall across the street. In 1850, when Paris began fortifying itself with a new encircling wall, the rue de Bagnolet was deemed a vital north-south supply route, and it was widened and graded for military use. Further down the hill is the village center and the church of St-Germain de Charonne on the hillside above the Place St-Blaise. An 1836 painting shows the Charonne town hall in front of

the church before it was demolished when the road was widened. The church is one of only two left in Paris with its own cemetery. The other one is in Montmartre. The cemetery once surrounded the church. The village center then was down the rue St-Blaise. The legend is that St-Germain, then the bishop

Etienne Bouhot, Church and Town Hall of Charonne, 1836, Pavillon de l'Hermitage

of Auxerre, baptized a six-year-old girl in the chapel here in the year 429. The girl became St-Geneviève, the patron saint of Paris. The church was closed in 2009 because of unstable walls. Steel beams supporting the outside walls can be seen from the street. During the

St-Germain de Charonne

rebuilding, excavations under the church have uncovered artifacts from eight centuries. The church is expected to be reopened in 2015. Walk down the tiny rue St-Blaise. It looks like a quaint Utrillo painting. Cheap rents have spawned several artists' ateliers here, but some new trendy cafés signal a possible gentrification and the end of low rent. At the end of the old part of the street is the Place

Rue St-Blaise

Place des Grès

des Grès, looking a little forgotten—maybe frozen in time. A gallows in the square dispensed justice in prerevolutionary days. The far left political climate of this working class quarter is embodied by the neighborhood headquarters of the Communist Party on the square across from the Magnolia Bar.

Parti Communiste HQ

Walk back up to the Place St-Blaise and turn left. If you're feeling extra energetic, walk up the hill next to the church to the cemetery. If not, continue down the right side of the rue de Bagnolet. The street crosses a bridge over railroad tracks. Look across the street at a dilapidated building with an awning that reads La Flèche d'Or. Look closer at the dark sign un-

Gare de Charonne, Street View

derneath and attached to the building reading CEINTURE. This was the Charonne station of the Petite Ceinture, the little beltway. After it was abandoned, it was a night club for a while called La Flèche d'Or. (The Golden Arrow was the name of a London to Paris boat train that ran from the 1930s to the 1970s.) There are always children running in and out of the railway tunnels despite the no trespassing warnings. Stations in the grittier neighborhoods, primarily in Eastern Paris, have become magnets for graffiti artists.

Down rue de Bagnolet at number 85 is the Villa Godin. The term villa doesn't necessarily mean anything luxurious. Generally they are gated lanes with tiny houses, in this case like attached cottages. We were trying to peek through the locked gate when an

Villa Godin

older woman who was going in invited us to see the houses. She told us

L'Escargot d'Or

she had lived there since 1970 and would never move. I checked prices on the web. These tiny houses are expensive! Further down the street is a former restaurant, l'Escargot d'Or, (the golden snail) with an oversized example above the door. It is now a coffee shop.

This is one of the easiest walking tours. It's mostly downhill. There are good places to eat. And along the rue de Bagnolet we can hop on the No 76 bus that runs along the rue de Rivoli back to the Louvre.

PASSY AND AUTEUIL

These two villages are often spoken of together. They are adjacent to each other along the Seine; Passy across from the Eiffel Tower, and Auteuil to the south. They are both considered upper class enclaves, although Passy feels and looks wealthy while Auteuil, with just as much wealth, just feels more folksy and cozy. Maybe

Boundry Marker on rue Berton

it's like Manhattan's Upper West Side and Upper East Side, two wealthy enclaves with different personalities. The ancient border between their *seigneuries* (lords of the manor) is marked by a *borne* or plaque affixed to a wall on the tiny rue Berton. Like most of the ancient countryside around Paris, both Passy and Auteuil were once the domains of monks.

AUTEUIL

Auteuil was a verdant plain above the Seine. Owned by the Abby of St-Geneviève before the revolution, it was noted for its hot springs and

Métro Porte d'Auteuil

excellent wine. To start the walk, take the No 10 Métro to the porte d'Auteuil. Take the 3rd exit to the rue d'Auteuil. The métro sign, in a pale green, is in the Art Nouveau style, popular at the turn of the nineteenth century. There are several

great examples of Art Nouveau in Auteuil. At the métro exit is the Gare d'Auteuil, a white two story building from the era of the Petite Ceinture. The well-off quarters in the west of Paris often had buffets in the stations. A trendy restaurant, Mary Goodnight, now occupies the space.

Gare d'Auteuil

The raised tracks behind the station have been abandoned. On the right side of the station, on the corner of the boulevard Montmorency and the rue Poussin, is a delightful village café, Le Beaujolais d'Auteuil. Dinner size portions at lunchtime include smoked salmon salads, veal kidneys, duck breast, and farm raised chicken. The wine selection features several cru's of the Beaujolais region. Take the rue

Le Beaujolais d'Auteuil

Poussin, which is to the left. It's a quiet street with several stand-alone homes, many of which are disappearing as new apartment blocks are built. After No 14 on the left side of the street, there is a gate with a

Private Home in Auteuil

guard house. Behind it are leafy trees and view of some gables on the roof line of homes. This is the Villa de Montmorency, a *quartier cossu privé*, or gated community. In 1853 the railroad bought up property in Auteuil anticipating construction of the Petite Ceinture and the station in Auteuil. The unused portion of land was developed in 1860. One hundred and twenty homes were built on spacious lots. Many were designed to replicate seaside villas in resort towns like Deauville. The rich and famous quickly moved in, and its popularity has never waned. A few years ago, Céline Dion was reported to have paid forty-seven million Euros for her Paris pied-à-terre. Recently there has been a case of the blues in the "millionaire's ghetto." Wealthy CEO's and movie stars like Gérard Depardieu have left

Villa Montmorency

France for other tax venues such as Belgium because of a new 75 percent tax on millionaires. No one outside the villa seems to be worried about the falling prices. The incongruity is that the neighborhood around it is middle class. Maybe it acts as camouflage to distract the curious. Take the short street across from the gate to the Place Jean Lorrain, with a Wallace fountain in the center.

Wallace Fountain, Auteuil

I recommend a short side trip from the Place Jean Lorrain along the rue Jean de La Fontaine that features, among other treasures, a major Art Nouveau architectural wonder. The walk is a pleasant one and you can always take the No 52 bus back to the rue d'Auteuil.

Henri Sauvage Ateliers

AT number 65 is an imposing modern building that houses artists' ateliers. It was designed by Henri Sauvage and finished in 1927. Its style is described as Art Déco, but the the stark lines of the ceramic tile exterior give it more of a cubist look.

A two story brown stone building stands at number 40. On one side is a military looking turret, on the other, the entrance to a gothic cloister. Behind the building is the extensive campus of the Apprentis d'Auteuil. Founded in 1866 by a priest, Father Louis Roussel, as an orphanage, it has grown over time to a large insti-

Cloister at Apprentis d'Auteuil

tution serving over 9,000 poor and orphaned children in multiple locations, training them in culinary arts and the hospitality sector. A beautiful chapel on the grounds is dedicated to St-Thérèse de Lisieux, where her relics are kept. There is a statue nearby of Father Daniel Brottier, the second director of the institution.

Father Daniel Brottier

Standing with a street urchin on his shoulders, he looks curiously like Father Flanagan of Boys Town.

At number 60 is the Hôtel Mezzara, a mansion built in 1910 by Hector Guimard, the master of Art Nouveau, for Paul Mezzara, a Venetian textile magnate. It fills the entire space except for a tiny courtyard in the front. It is severely asymmetrical, but it all comes together

Hotel Mezzara

with soft lines, superb iron work, and sculpted stone flowers.

The grand masterpiece of Art Nouveau is further down the street at number 14. The Castel Béranger was the apex of the movement. It

Castel Beranger

Castel Beranger Entrance

was finished in 1898. It was radical. The Surrealist movement would begin twenty years later, but this could have been a part of it. It was quickly derided as the Castel Dérangé (disturbed). Guimard was only twenty-seven when he started construction on it. It became famous enough for Guimard to get the commission to design over thirty ornamental métro kiosks. In the Castel Béranger, curvy lines are followed by sharp angles. The lack of symmetry prevails. Windows cascade down walls of red brick. Each of the thirty-six apartments has a unique floor plan. It is simply hard to describe it, or to even photograph in its entirety. Go see it! Up the street at number 17 is a tiny bar designed by Guimard, the Café Antoine, complete with a stone fox above the door.

It's good for a drink or a sandwich. Because Art Nouveau fell out of favor so quickly, nearly all of Guimard's métro station designs and several of his buildings have been destroyed.

Café Antoine

Hôtel de Verrières

Walk back to the Place Jean Lorrain, or ride the No 52 bus. Turn left on the rue d'Auteuil. From here, the village ambience of Auteuil becomes more intense. At number 42 there is a stylish white building called the Hôtel de Verrières. It was built for a celebrated opéra singer Mademoiselle Antier, and was later offered to *les demoiselles de Ver-*

rières, young opéra singers, by their royal protectors. It now houses a law office. At number 40 is the Auberge du Mouton Blanc, identified by the sign of the white sheep above the door. Dating back to the 1600s, it counted among its regulars Molière, Racine,

Auberge Le Mouton Blanc, Auteuil

and La Fontaine, who lived in Auteuil. Its rough stone walls are original, but the interior has been updated. It is a good place to stop for lunch. From here until the end of the rue d'Auteuil, there is more of a nineteenth century feel. On the right hand side, several three story buildings have odd looking gables on their roofs with beams for pulleys extending from them. Large objects were required to hoist the narrow stairs up to the second floor. I have never seen these in other parts of Paris. The shopkeepers here are local. There are no luxury boutiques. At the end of the street is the Place de l'Eglise, dominated

Notre-Dame d'Auteuil

by the Church of Notre-Dame d'Auteuil. It was built in 1877, replacing one that had grown too small for the population. The old church had been surrounded by its own cemetery, which was removed when the current church was built. It is in the Roman-Byzantine style and has a fifty meter bell tower. An obelisk across from the church, placed there under Louis XIV, honors Henri-François d'Aguesseau, a chancellor of France. On the side of square is a chapel built by the church to honor St-Bernadette, and across the square are hospital grounds that include the former Auteuil town hall among its buildings. This is one of the

best laid out squares in all of the old villages. The Art Nouveau Métro entrance completes the picture. The No 10 Métro runs east-west across Paris and connects with most other lines. The 32 bus runs from here back to the Opéra.

Auteuil, place de l'Eglise

Gabled building on rue d'Auteuil

Auteuil Skyline

On the rue d'Auteuil

Chocolatier on rue d'Auteuil

Métro Eglise d'Auteuil

PASSY

Passy was first chartered as a hamlet called "Passicium" in the year 1250. During the same period, limestone was quarried on the hills leading down to the Seine, and then carried by boat to central Paris. The mines extended miles into the hills below Passy. Over time the stone proved too porous for building and the quarries were abandoned. In the 15th century, an order of monks, the Menims, settled in Passy. They used the abandoned mines to store the wines they made from their vineyards that covered the hills of Passy. The mines are now part of the Musée du Vin on the tiny square Charles Dickens. Windmills once dotted the hills amid orchards. The Château de Boulainvilliers stood at the southern end of Passy near the border with Auteuil. It no longer exists; its land was developed for a residential neighborhood.

The Passy walk begins near a tiny former station of the Petite Ceinture. The Passy station is now a restaurant, La Gare. It is visible from La Muette stop on the No 9 Métro. Take the number 1 exit for the Chausée de la Muette. You are immediately surrounded by four elegant Haussemann style apartment buildings, a sign of what's to come. The brick and stone station will be on the left at the edge of a triangular park called the Jardin du Ranelagh.

Gare de Passy

The old track right of way behind the station is now a walking trail. Head in the direction away from the park back toward the métro. The street changes name to the rue de Passy, the main street of the affluent village where

Walking trail behind the Gare de Passy

Rue de Passy

the "gratin" (upper crust) of the 16th Arrondissement do their daily shopping. The main street looks like anything but a village. The rue de Passy is lined with designer boutiques on both sides of the street. Passy has its own little shopping mall, the Passy Plaza, filled with more boutiques, and its own department store, Franck et Fils, on the rue de Passy. As you pass the Passy Plaza, take the small street on the right, the rue Jean Bologne, keep right toward the church. The Eglise Notre-Dame de Grâce de Passy sits on a tree-filled square. The en-

trance is around the back of the church on the rue de l'Annonciation. A chapel with the same name was built here in 1667 by Claude Chahu, Lord of Passy. In the eighteen hundreds, it was enlarged several times to its present size. The parish grew so fast in the 1900s that a new church was built next to

Passy Plaza

it on the rue de l'Annonciation in 1959 that holds 1200 worshipers. The old church was renovated and reopened in 1997. Continue down

Notre-Dame de Grâce de Passy

the rue de l'Annonciation past some low 18th century buildings to the rue Raynouard. Turn right. At number 47 on the side of a hill is the Maison Balzac, where Honoré de Balzac lived from 1840 to 1847. He fled the city to

Passy and this humble house to escape creditors. There he edited his *Human Comedy*, the master work that brought him fame and fortune. The home is open to visitors.

Maison Balzac Gate

Head back down the rue de Passy. Further on the right is a small square, the Place de Passy with a Wallace fountain and a terraced restaurant. To the right of the square is the Marché de Passy, a high-end indoor market where the best meat, fish, fruits, vegetables, cheese, and herbs are offered to the demanding Passyites. On the right, among more boutiques, is La Favorite, a restaurant where I had one of the best warm goat cheese salads ever. But there is a more authentic village place further down the rue de Passy. On the left, between the numbers 26 and 24, is the Impasse des Carrières. At the end of the short lane is a *brocante*, an antique market under old oak beams with curios for everyone. Next to it, behind vine-covered walls, is the Villa de Passy, a genial restaurant. Outdoor tables under an awning were filled with happy locals on the Saturday I walked by. In the local patois it is "*très sympa*" or very pleasant. Further down the street is the Place Costa Rica, which marks the end of the rue de Passy. Stand in the square and look down the rue de l'Alboni where the No 6 Métro travels on its elevated tracks on

View from rue de l'Alboni

the left bank across the Bir-Hakeim Bridge and into the hillside of Passy. Follow the rue Benjamin Franklin which veers slightly to the left. Ben Franklin lived in Passy during the American Revolution. He was sent to convince King Louis XV to support the colonies against England, their

Place de Passy

La Favorite

Marché de Passy

Villa de Passy

joint enemy. As the street goes downhill, stay to the left to follow the rue Benjamin Franklin. At the bottom of the hill is the Square de

Yorktown, a tiny park that surrounds a statue of Benjamin Franklin. A plaque commemorates the battle of Yorktown in 1781, when American troops led by George Washington and French troops led by General Rochambeau defeated the British led by General Cornwallis, leading to his surrender and the end of the war. Few Americans are aware of the French participation. Walk around the Palais de Chaillot for a great view of

Square de Yorktown, Benjamin Franklin

the Eiffel Tower. The No 6 Métro stops at the Trocadéro and the 82 bus stops at the avenue d'Iéna on the other side.

LA PETITE CEINTURE, THE LITTLE RAILWAY THAT CONNECTED THE VILLAGES

As France began building railways to reach all of the country's frontiers in 1837, the stations were built around the periphery of the city toward the direction they served. For example the Gare du Nord was in the north of Paris. The Gare Montparnasse, which served the southwest, was on that edge of the city. By 1846, Paris had six major railway stations serving all regions of France. This Paris centric model was fine for Parisians. They could go anywhere. But freight crossing the country in a north-south or east-west direction had to be unloaded at one station in Paris , then hauled through a busy city to another station on horse drawn carriages. Not very efficient. When Napoléon III came to power in 1851, he decided that by linking the train stations of Paris he could unite France. There was a military rationale as well. Between 1841 and 1844 a defensive wall was built around Paris outside the city limits. It was named for Adolphe Thiers, then the prime minister. The new emperor's idea was that a circular railway could quickly marshal resources to any part of the fortifications in case of attack. The first arc in the circle connected two freight yards in the north of Paris. In 1854 as the circle began taking shape, passenger stations were added every several miles and by 1869 the belt (*ceinture*) of thirty-six stations was complete. Since the railway was built just inside the Thiers wall, it ran through the villages that surrounded Paris. The city expanded its borders in 1860 by annexing these villages. At the same time, Baron Haussmann, Napoléon's architect, was cutting wide boulevards across the city that spawned new residential development. The beltway united the new neighborhoods, particularly in western Paris where the building boom was driving construction of elegant apartment buildings. Most of the tiny stations were at street level. The two tracks ran on the surface in some areas. In others, they ran in short tunnels, or below ground level, in an uncovered trench. A few sections were elevated above the street. Considering that there were no motorized trucks or buses, the steam locomotives circled the city quite efficiently for both freight and passengers.

Train on la Petite Ceinture, ca 1910

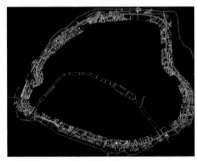

Route of La Petite Ceinture

The Paris métro changed everything. The first one came on line in 1900, crossing the city underground in an east-west axis. Over the next ten years, ten more métro lines were built, connecting all quarters and railway stations of the city. They ran on electricity instead of coal. New national rail lines allowed for cross country trains to bypass Paris. The Thiers wall was dismantled in the 1920s. The Petite Ceinture had lost its usefulness and was closed in 1937. The rail right of way fell into disrepair and the tiny stations ended up in various states of disuse. Someone must have noticed that the right of way width exactly matched that of a tennis court, so in the nicer western Paris neighborhoods tennis clubs sprung up with courts laid end to end. Elsewhere, walking trails and New York style high lines have succeeded the railways. The ultimate fate of the closed stations depended on which side of Paris they were located. The traditional delineation of Paris is on a Right Bank-Left Bank orientation, which is more of a north-south divide. Economically, and politically, however, the city has long been divided on an east-west basis. Working class neighborhoods in the eastern part of Paris were some of the oldest and grittiest. Western Paris was opened up under Haussemann during the time that the Petite Ceinture was being built. The stations in the west were elegantly placed in their neighborhoods and are all still in use, some as stations for new commuter lines and others as tony restaurants. In the east, the stations were built of brick instead of stone, and have all been abandoned. Some have been destroyed. Most are covered with graffiti and sit in iffy quarters, sad and scowling with no purpose in life. But all this is changing. Recently new interest in these forgotten relics has led to efforts to recycle some of them and the right of way for popular use.

Of the thirty-six stations of the Petite Ceinture, eighteen have been destroyed. Batignoles is still used by the French railroad as a stop after the Gare St-Lazare, but it was never actually in the Batignoles village. It is called the Gare du Pont Cardinet.

Gare du pont Cardinet

The Gare de Vaugirard may get a new life since the elevated tracks

Gare de Vaugirard

have been modified as a mile long, high line walk way. The three story brick building has held office tenants and has avoided the graffiti that has plagued other abandoned stations. The stations of avenue de St-Ouen and Charonne are

Gare St-Ouen

in such a bad state they can hardly be identified from the busy streets they sit on. Only in the back, where the below-street level tracks offer a glimpse of the rear of the station, does the colorful graffiti illuminate what once were busy terminals. The Gare Ornano was repurposed in 2014. There is a casual bar and restaurant in the station itself, and you can picnic on tables quai beside the tracks. It is popular with young people and may actually improve the livability of this run-down neighborhood. The Gare de Montrouge is in the process of being restored as commercial and restaurant space as part of neighborhood beautification projects. The Gare

Gare de Charonne

de Paris-Ouest is used as office space by the Société Nationale des Chemins de fer Français (French National Railways [SNCF]), the national railroad. Two other stations, the Gare d'Orléans and the Gare de Flandre, are graffiti covered and inaccessible to the public. It is in the wealthier western part of the city that the six remaining stations

Gare Ornano 2013

Gare Ornano 2014

Gare Ornano New Restaurant & Bar

Gare d'Orléans

Gare Montrouge Restoration

Gare de Neuilly-porte Maillot

shine. They were built to blend in with the grand architecture of the era. They have all been repurposed. The gares de Passy and Auteuil are both popular restaurants. The Neuilly-porte Maillot station, standing proudly on the busy Place de la porte Maillot, is now a station of the RER commuter line. The Gare de l'avenue du bois du Boulogne was built for the 1900 Universal Exhibition in the monumental style to receive the heads of state of Spain and

Gare de Passy

Italy. It is now called the Gare de l'avenue Foch of the RER line. Its below grade tracks have been covered and a line of tennis courts follow the old right of way. The Gare de Courcelles-Levallois followed a similar pattern. Sitting on the sunny Place Pereire, it was built in 1854 and was expanded to four tracks for the 1900 Universal Exhibition. It closed in 1925. The below grade tracks were covered in 1984 as it transitioned to the RER suburban line. It too is trailed by a series of tennis courts in this exquisite neighborhood.

Gare Henri Martin

If I could be any station of the Petite Ceinture today, I would be the Gare Henri Martin. Positioned at the end of avenue Victor Hugo where the avenue Henri Martin meets the boulevard Flandrin at the tiny Place Tattegrain, it has the best of all worlds. Built with pink brick trimmed with cut stone, it looks out over the peaceful square. The front of the station and its broad terrace is the home of the restaurant Le Flandrin, where the well-heeled come to be well fed. It is a place to see and be seen in the most expensive neighborhood in the 16th Arrondissement. The restaurant's voiturier parks clients' Italian sports cars—the kind whose names end in a vowel. The average Parisian probably never walks in this neighborhood. Le Café Flandrin is known for its classic menu as well as for the people watching. It's hard to believe that it's actually a working station of the RER commuter line. The station part is in the back of the building and accessible from the side. The tracks behind the station are now covered, and the space is used for parking.

Given the current wave of nostalgia in Paris for the old railroad, I doubt that any more of the remaining stations will be destroyed, although some will have to wait their turn at being recycled and repurposed. The high line concept is catching on in other neighborhoods in Paris as well, and I expect that there will be further development of the abandoned stations and the rail right of way.

Gare de l'avenue Foch

Gare de Courcelles-Levallois

Le Flandrin

Bar at Petit Villiers

Bouillion Chartier, serving hungry workers every day since 1896

CHAPTER 8

Favorites

Friends who are going to Paris often ask, "What's your favorite restaurant?" Our answer is, "It depends." Ernest Hemingway, during the days of literary Montparnasse, said in *A Moveable Feast*, "Everyone had their private cafés where they never invited anyone and would go to work, or to read or to receive their mail. They had other cafés where they would meet their mistresses and almost everyone had another café, a neutral café, where they might invite you to meet their mistress and there were regular, convenient, cheap dining places where everyone might eat on neutral ground." Over time, I came to understand what he meant, not the mistress part, but the situational nature of choosing where to go, or which to recommend, so I'll channel Hemingway with our situational favorites.

Everyone should have a place, close by, where they know you and treat you like old friends and is a perfect example of what a restaurant should be, a place where you dine every week or two, and where you take visiting friends to give them an example of an intimate, but relaxed, Parisian restaurant where food is taken seriously. This is Le Florimond at 19 avenue de la Motte-Picquet. It was opened in 1993 by a young Pascal Guillaumin, a product of three generations of farmers and charcutiers from the Corrèze region. His lineage is reflected in the restaurant's theme, "Recipes of my grandmother." He was recently designated a Master Restaurateur of France based on the quality of ingredients, expertise of cooking, service, and ambience. Like many great chefs, he began his apprenticeship at age sixteen. Le Florimond is named after the master gardener at Giverny, Monet's home in Normandy, to evoke the use of textures, colors, and flavors. This alone would give Le Florimond a dedicated word-of-mouth following. Laurent, Pascal's partner since 1995, oversees the dining room with superb people skills that complement the food. Savvy visiting Americans who know Paris dine here whenever they are in town. They are seated among the Parisian regulars in the brightly lit room that holds a dozen or so tables. Laurent describes the day's offerings in both lan-

guages using humor that puts everyone at ease, as with old friends. Foie gras from Pascal's family farm in Corrèze, le *chou farci* (stuffed cabbage) from his grandmother's recipe and other regular menu items are com-

Le Florimond

bined with seasonal choices, making up a daily prix fixe formula that includes unforgettable desserts. The menu and the wine choices are all moderately priced. Reservations are a must.

Everyone should also have a place that is nearby where they can go morning, noon, or night without a reservation and with little or no wait, be seated at a table. The menu will have predictable standard

dishes as well as quick choices like omelets, salads, quiches, onion soup, and croque-monsieurs, all at reasonably low prices. It's nine o'clock on Sunday night and we decide we're hungry. We walk to La Terrasse. It takes up the entire corner of avenue Bosquet and avenue de la Motte-Picquet and has dining rooms on two floors as well as a broad out-

La Terrasse

door terrace. Its young, busy, efficient wait staff navigate among the tables, wasting no time in bringing carafes of wine and water with the plats du jour. As busy as it is, there is never any feeling of being hurried. It is usually packed equally with locals and visitors alike.

A SPECIAL PLACE FOR DINNER

Then there is dinner on a special occasion, with a special person, a once or twice a year kind of place for an anniversary or birthday to celebrate à *deux*. For some, maybe a once in a lifetime experience on a Paris vacation. More than a favorite restaurant, it is a favorite evening. It is Lasserre at 17 avenue Franklin Roosevelt, one of the most

beloved gastronomic institutions in Paris. In 1942, René Lasserre purchased the small building left over from the World's Fair of 1937. After the war he opened the Club de la Casserole, the place to see and be seen after society events, and won

Lasserre

his first Michelin star. In 1951 the building was renovated to today's incarnation of a small, white stucco two story mansion. It became Lasserre. A second star was awarded the next year. At the door you are greeted by the host and ushered into a private elevator by the maître d' and escorted to the second floor dining room. As you exit the elevator and enter the chandeliered belle époque dining room, there is a feeling that you should be formally announced. The room is bright and full of flower arrangements. In pleasant weather the roof is opened to the stars. From eight o'clock on, guests arrive. A coat is re-

Lasserre dining room

quired for men. Women are fashionably attired. (We lament the death of the dress code in the U.S., which has resulted in an anything-goes jeans and sneakers culture.) The décor and dress are in keeping with the exceptional evening ahead. At your table, canapés are served with small crispy loaves that beg to be spread with the rich, *demi-sel*, Bordier butter. A pianist in the corner softly plays "As time goes by" (because I requested it!). Then, a flûte de champagne to start and a look at the menu: classic first courses like penne stuffed with black truffles and foie gras, or cold lobster bisque, then main courses of tournedos Rossini, grilled bonito, Bresse chicken, and wild duck. One dessert especially intrigued us—peaches poached in wine with wild strawberries under a meringue dôme. Wines are recommended with the choice of courses. Upon finishing the meal, the ladies are presented with a tiny porcelain saucepan as a souvenir. Even though the evening can cost three or four times as much as one at a moderately priced restaurant, we will continue our semiannual pilgrimage.

SUNDAY LUNCH

Sunday lunch at a restaurant in Paris is an institution originating from the era when Sunday was the servants' day off. It is unlike any other meal. Entire families sit down at around one o'clock for a two or three hour meal usually starting with aperitifs and ending with dessert and coffee. This is not the American version of brunch and Bloody Marys, although some cafés where twentysomethings congregate have begun serving what they call "le brunch" on weekends, looking more like an American breakfast. Many restaurants in Paris close on Sunday. Those that remain open go all out to make Sunday lunch a special event, with seasonal prix fixe menus that frequently include an aperitif, three courses, wine, and coffee. The atmosphere is jovial with clinking glasses and lively conversation. Each restaurant seems to have its own local following. When we are in Paris, we rotate our choice for Sunday lunch among several favorites depending on our mood, the season, and proximity to whichever museum or neighborhood we plan to visit. Sometimes we take in an afternoon concert and we choose a trusted place close by. All of these upscale places are great for lunch or dinner any day of the week, but we save them for Sunday.

Aérogare des Invalides

In the fall and winter, we always make sure to have at least one Sunday lunch at Au Petit Marguery located at 9 boulevard Port-Royal. A bright red awning in front welcomes their followers into a classic traditional mirrored dining room. It is busy year round, but the fall and winter menus bring out the wild game connoisseurs for a convivial Sunday lunch. Oysters, mushrooms, chestnuts, and root vegetables all figure into their menus featuring partridge, hare, venison, and wild boar, all served in a friendly atmosphere.

Au Petit Marguery

Because of its hidden location behind and beneath the Aérogare des Invalides, with its own terrace, Chez Françoise seems to be known only to Parisians. A small train station was commissioned in 1900 on the northeast side of the grassy Esplanade des Invalides. It served a short line railroad that went to Versailles. Rail serviced was discontinued in 1935. In 1949, Air France opened a shuttle bus terminal in the old station to serve the first air travellers going to and from Orly Airport where they could purchase tickets, check their baggage, and enjoy elegant dining. Chez Françoise was born. Being around the corner from the National Assembly made it a choice for politicians too, and many deals have been done in its private dining rooms. It became fashionable for well-connected folks to be seen here Sunday afternoons. On our first visit, one spring Sunday afternoon, we were welcomed like old friends and have never forgotten it. Their Sunday menu is extensive and at reasonable fixed prices.

Chez Françoise

Christian Constant is one of the brightest stars of the Parisian food scene. His flagship restaurant, the modern Violon d'Ingres at

Le Violon d'Ingres

135 rue St-Dominique, earned a Michelin star soon after it opened. He recently gave up the star to focus on a more accessible and less pretentious menu. His followers responded by filling the dining room every day, so reservations are a must. On Sundays he prepares a special three course meal that is both elegant and complex. It is on our rotating list for Sunday lunch.

The Auberge Dab at 161 avenue Malakoff is hidden from the nearby busy porte Maillot traffic circle by a topiary hedge that puts it in another time and place. Brown leather and polished wood banquettes, silk curtains, and a carved staircase remind me of a luxury cruise ship dining room of the 1930s. On Sundays it fills with families celebrating their

Auberge Dab

weekly reunion. There is a general ambience of contentment in the dining room as the wait staff deftly attends to each table. The covered terrace is open from April through September.

On the Sundays we are hungry for seafood, we head to Le Dôme at 108 on the boulevard Montparnasse. It was the first of the celebrated cafés in the neighborhood when it opened in 1898. It witnessed the arrival of artists from Montmartre in the 1900s and the literary crowd from the U.S. in the 1920s. Its Michelin star testifies to the fact that its following is not

Le Dôme

just due to history or décor. It is a temple of seafood, and on Sundays, locals feast on fresh shellfish, bouillabaisse, and our favorite, sole meunière. A Sunday-only mille-feuille pastry is a must-have for us, but just one slice with two spoons! Varnished wood around the booths, brass plaques dedicated to the *Domiers,* as the artists and writer habitués were known, add to the experience.

Another seafood experience awaits at La Mediterranée. It opened in 1942, at 2 Place de l'Odeon, and attracted established artists and writer friends of the owner. Christian Bérard painted bright murals. Cocteau's lithographs alternate with them. La Mediterranée states that it "remains a circumspect meeting place for some of the most popular figures in art and literature." We didn't know any of this

La Méditerranée

when we first tried it for Sunday lunch. What we discovered is that it's a perfect place for delicately prepared fresh fish. It is brighter and lighter than Le Dôme, and its tables look out from the dining room on the Théâtre de l'Odéon near the Luxembourg Gardens. Starter selections include several fish carpaccios, white asparagus in the summer and langouste salads, followed by main courses of wild turbot, sea bream "lacquered" with honey, and their own take on bouillabaisse. It is the alter ego to the wood paneled Dôme.

The last one on our list, and way outside the moderate category, is Benoît at 20 rue St-Martin near the Hôtel de Ville. It was opened by Benoît Matray in 1912 and stayed in the family until it was acquired by Alain Ducasse who states, "There's no other place in Paris as typically Parisian as Benoît … a friendly place, full of memories

and shared pleasure." Everything about it evokes the past: etched glass partitions between the tables, velvet seats, brass fixtures. Ducasse, an already acclaimed chef, took the bistro food genre to new levels and earned a Michelin star. The menu features country casseroles, foie gras, pork loin, and seasonal choices

Sunday lunch at Benoît

like pheasant, autumn terrines, and the unbelievable lamb tenderloin we shared one Sunday in the spring. An extensive wine list covers all regions and price ranges. Portions are generous in the bistro tradition, including the desserts like Savarin, (a brown cake) doused with Armagnac, profiteroles, and Pears Belle Hélène. Waitstaff in black vests and ties complete the "I feel like I'm in a French movie!" fantasy.

OUT AND ABOUT AT LUNCHTIME

As we explore the city, we always try to find an authentic neighborhood restaurant, maybe a café, bistro, or brasserie that attracts local working people as well as retired couples (like us), who are having their main meal of the day. We peruse the menu displayed out front, check the façade for the authentic patina that is found on a neighborhood gem, and then listen for the noise that is generated by

Galerie Vero-Dodat

satisfied people enjoying great food. Our list has grown to the point that we have go-to places in all parts of Paris. It's possible to walk in without a reservation in these places, but as they are popular, it is wise to call ahead, or get there before one o'clock.

1st ARRONDISSEMENT

The Café de l'Epoque has the added attraction of sitting in the Galerie Véro-Dodat which connects the rue de Jean-Jacques Rousseau and the rue du Bouloi near the Palais Royal. This neoclassical passage now contains luxury and artisanal shops, most notably Christian Louboutin, famous for his red-soled ladies shoes. Black and white tiles, columns, frescoes, and warm wood storefronts

Café de l'Epoque at the Galerie Vero-Dodat

make the Galerie Véro-Dodat a perfect place for lunch and window shopping. The restaurant, at 2 rue Buloi, is in the same design with 1930s décor. Starters like *oeuf* (eggs) *mayonnaise* and foie gras, combined with main courses of *blanquette de veau* and low cost wines make it a gem, popular with shoppers and local workers.

Chez Flottes, at 2 rue Cambon, is near the Place de la Concorde, just off the rue de Rivoli and away from all the souvenir shops. A re-

cent article in *Le Figaro* rated its *poulet rôti frites* (roast chicken with fries) in the top ten in Paris. Although it always seems busy, we are shown to a table right away and our poulet arrives quickly. A perfect lunch place for the busy shopper.

Chez Flottes

2nd ARRONDISEMENT

The Brasserie Le Vaudeville faces the Paris *Bourse* (stock exchange) at 29 rue Vivienne. It is not a place for a quick bite at midday. It is a classic brasserie with etched glassed panels separating the rooms and

plenty of polished brass. The staff caters to lovers of seafood with platers of crustaceans sitting atop beds of shaved ice. The prices are in the moderate range. If you have the time and budget for a memorable lunchtime experience, try it.

Le Vaudeville

Le Tambour is at No 41 on the same street, but it's very different in many ways. First, it is a two story half-timbered building from another age that appears to be stuck onto the end of a modern apartment house. Second, it never closes, day or night,

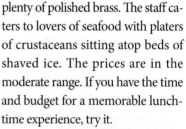

Le Tambour

making it popular with after-concert goers and other late nighters. The offering is uncomplicated standards: steak au poivre, goat cheese salads, escargot, terrines, and onion soup. Here, prices are on the lower side, which keeps the place busy.

3rd ARRONDISSEMENT

If you are in the Place des Vosges in the Marais, head across the square from the rue de Birague entrance. Take the rue de Béarn, then

Chez Janou

the first right onto the rue Roger Verlomme. At the end of the block is Chez Janou. They specialize in the cuisine of Provence. On warm evenings the square in front is full of fans drinking apéritifs as they wait for a table. Tapenade, ratatouille, and fresh salads make this a favorite stop for lunch when we are in the Marais.

The French have a name for it. *Cuisine ménagère*—home cooking. That's what you'll find at Chez Nénesse on the corner of the rue

Saintonge and the rue de Poitou. The décor is simple and functional, kind of a 1950s retro. The scene unfolds as Chef Roger Leplu, wife Chantal, and son Cyrille execute the ballet moves at lunchtime to serve classic dishes from their

Chez Nenesse

daily menu to the daily crowds. My brother, on a week's visit, my wife and I arrived at 12:45, our strategy for getting a table before the rush. We ordered from the chalkboard, something different for each of us. For entrées, the *assiette de crudities*, finely shredded carrots, celery root, and diced red beets, covered in thick vinaigrette; *céleri remoulade*, celery root in mayonnaise, and *poireaux vinaigrette*, a braised leek with the same vinaigrette. All exquisitely simple. For our main dishes: sautéed turkey breast with boiled potatoes, pork shoulder with green lentils, and a grilled steak with lovely green beans. While we were still on our main courses, I caught the eye of Chantal and quietly asked her to set aside some of the dessert de jour, apple custard *clafoutis,* before it was gone. She did, with a smile, and it was exceptional.

4th ARRONDISSEMENT

When we are near the old Jewish quarter in the 4th Arrondissment, I never miss eating at l'As du Fallafel at 32-34 rue des Rosiers.

A long line usually forms at the sidewalk service window for their famous falafel sandwich. We go inside instead and order the heathier falafel platter that includes the sesame cream, veggies, and lamb or chicken. Israeli beer or kosher wine are both good pairings.

L'As du Fallafel

There is something about the Brasserie de l'Ile St-Louis, on the tip of the Isle St-Louis, just across the bridge connecting it to the Ile de la Cité. It draws you in on a wintry day like a country auberge. The curtained windows, the long tables, the hunting trophies, the mature, brusque (some say grumpy) waiters, combine to create a perfect, unstaged setting for

Brasserie de l'Ile St-Louis

enjoying Alsacian food. Pork is big here: pig's knuckles with lentils and *choucroute garnie*—French kraut steemed in Riesling wine with several kinds of sausage. Steins of Mutzig beer from Alsace and pots of mustard on the table complete the experience.

Choucroute Garnie

Le Pré Verre

5th ARRONDISSEMENT

Comprising the Latin Quarter, major universities, and the monumental pantheon, the 5th Arrondissement does not lack for great places to lunch. It is worth sifting through the hundreds of choices though, to separate the student pizza and burger joints from the true haunts of academics, administrators, and professionals looking for a no-drama, tasty meal.

Le Pré Verre begins filling up well before one o'clock and is still going strong at three. They'll give you a written menu if you want one, but none of their regulars ever ask for one. They just look at the chalkboard and choose one of the daily specials. The starter was a creamy vegetable soup with a hint of cumin. The main course was a roasted *pintade* (guinea hen) over a bed of risotto. Wine and coffee were included in the low priced formula. Those on a short break for lunch can have a great midday meal here. The address is 8 rue Thénard.

Menu de Jour at Pré Verre

Chez Lina et Mimile

Chez Lina et Mimile overlooks the intersection of the rue Tournefort and the rue l'Homond at the bottom of the hill behind the Panthon. It's close to the touristy rue Mouffetard, but in a neighborhood setting never seen by tourists. The restaurant is actually a former home sitting on an elevated terrace above the tiny Place Luc-

Chez Lina et Mimile Interior

ien Herr. The tables on the terrace are shaded by red awnings and are packed with locals at lunch and dinner during the summer. The owners, Marie-Martine and Christelle, keep the spirit of this 1937 vintage place alive. Although French to its core, it offers Iberian ham along with old home favorites. I started with an amazing *courgette* (zucchini) tart. It was topped with a layer of thick cream mixed with garlic and dill. I continued with another starter, their country pâté. The wines by the glass are generous, both in their taste and the size of the pour. The address is 2 rue Tournefort.

6th ARRONDISSEMENT

There are several great lunch places in the St-Germain-des-Près neighborhood. Le Bistro Mazarin is at No 42 rue Mazarine. We've tak-en our grandchildren several times after a morning in the Luxembourg Garden playground. The ochre-toned interior and dark green leather banquettes gave a warm welcome. We shared a brie en croute to start, the children had roast chicken with frites. The adults had roast lamb and duck. For dessert we all shared a crème brûlée and an apple tart.

Le Bistro Mazarin

Polidor, at 41 rue Monsieur le Prince, near the Théâtre de l'Odéon, has been around since 1845. Their offerings have probably not changed since their opening and have been sampled by Victor Hugo,

Ernest Hemingway, Paul Ver-laine, and Arthur Rimbaud: escargot, *oeuf mayonnaise*, lamb with lentils, veal stew. In-expensive wines are available by the glass. Its façade appears in Woody Allen's *Midnight in Paris*.

Polidor

7th ARRONDISSEMENT

This is our section of town. The quiet streets are full of dependable mom and pop restaurants. We will never forget discovering Au Pied de Fouet at 45 rue de Babylone. It's down the street from La Pagode cinema, where we watch American and British movies shown in *version originale* (English). Au Pied de Fouet (the buggy whip) is possi-bly the tiniest restaurant in Paris, and one

Au Pied de Fouet

of the most authentic. It is in an ancient coach house that was once outside the city, hence the quaint name. It fills up quickly at lunch. We try to get in at 12:30 before the surge. Sometimes we are offered complementary after-lunch coffee if we take it at the bar to free the table for other hungry patrons.

The Bistro Le P'tit Troquet, tucked away on the tiny rue de l'Exposition, is the epitome of the one room neighborhood bistro. The

Le P'tit Troquet

quarter lies between the Eiffel Tower and the Invalides. Home cooking is the rule here: stuffed veal, cod with dill cream sauce, lamb brochette with garlic, rabbit leg with mushrooms. I remember a delightful pumpkin soup we had one October day. The menu changes every week.

8th ARRONDISSEMENT

The 8th Arrondissement is a land of extremes when it comes to restaurants. They are either very expensive or touristy burger and pizza joints. Our solution when faced with neighborhoods like this is to go to the side streets off the main squares to find were the real people eat. We love the place Madeleine, but it is full of high priced restaurants and boutiques. However, on the rue Vignon, which runs off of the right rear side of the church, there are several places where neighborhood folks go. We like Le Select Vignon at No 11. Their daily offerings are on a chalkboard out front. They would make anyone hungry: pork tenderloin with honey and mushrooms, salmon tartare, and steak with Roquefort sauce and zucchini.

Le Select Vignon

As we were walking through the Parc Monceau one October day, we began thinking about lunch. The area had a lot of offices and we watched well-dressed young professionals filing into Le Monceau, a

Le Monceau

restaurant that cuts through the triangle formed by the intersection of the rue de Lisbonne and the rue Monceau. It didn't look like a mom and pop kind of place. Soft gray tones, wall sconces and quiet conversations. We decided to try it. For starters, we shared an endive salad with bleu cheese and walnuts. Our main courses were duck breast with potatoes au gratin, and *blanquette de veau*, a lamb stew in a thick white sauce. I asked our server if the robust looking gentleman in charge was *le patron* (owner). "Yes," she said, "and that woman over there is *la patronne*." So, a mom and pop place after all. It actually has two street addresses, 37 rue Monceau or 41 rue Lisbonne.

9th ARRONDISSEMENT

Some of the oldest neighborhoods have the best local bistros and the 9th Arondissement is full of them. The area around the Drouot auction house has the big boisterous Bouillon Chartier where they've been feeding hungry workers great meals for two centuries. A low priced, extensive menu attracts all classes of Parisians who share tables as the brusque waiters rush to and from the kitchen. It is at No 7 on the rue du Faubourg-Montmartre.

Bouillon Chartier

Nearby in the banking district, at 43 rue Laffitte, is Le Laffitte where Claude Olivier greets lunch customers from behind the bar.

Hungry workers tend to overwhelm the place at around one o'clock. I try to get there early. "Table or bar?" he asks. He remembers every person waiting and after a few minutes shows them where to sit. Meat that melts in your

Le Laffitte

mouth is always on the plat du jour, complemented by some potato creation and green vegetables. I'll bet some folks eat here every day, and why not?

In the northern part of the 9th, near the Trinity church and the Musée de la Vie Romantique, is Chez Grenouille at 52 rue Blanche. We

Chez Grenouille

sometimes head to the neighborhood just to have lunch there. This very traditional bistro has a rustic aura. Seafood casseroles, asparagus with risotto, stuffed suckling pig, and their special sweetbreads with crème and morilles delight their followers.

10th ARRONDISSEMENT

The 10th Arrondissement borders the Canal St-Martin and its tree-lined promenade. It was featured in the movie *Amélie*. La Marine, at 55 bis quai de Valmy, overlooks the canal. The outdoor tables are filled on sunny afternoons. Seafood is the specialty here: avocado and shrimp tartare, fresh sea bass, and cod. Make this a stop on a stroll up or down the Canal St-Martin.

La Marine

At 57 rue de Lancry, on a corner just up the quai de Valmy, is Le Verre Volé (the stolen glass), a wine bar/wine store with a small kitchen that turns out small plates of crispy shrimp, sausage, paté, and salads. It has become very popular in this hip neighborhood.

Le Verre Volé

11ᵗʰ ARRONDISSEMENT

The Clown Bar at 114 rue Amelot is a tribute to the Cirque d'Hiver that sits next to it. It fills up at lunchtime on Wednesdays and week-

Clown Bar

ends before the circus matinées. The old school façade hides a newly brightened interior featuring vintage circus scenes. Clown portraits are everywhere. This is a cool place for adults to have lunch or dinner even if there are no plans to go to the circus. A new chef has introduced a more creative menu: grilled pork, squid, fresh fish, and pasta. They are open early and late.

As you approach Chez Paul, at 13 rue de Charonne, you may be put off by the sight of the worn signs and the faded awning. Disregard them and enter anyway! This is the epitome of a classic old French bistro. The menu is extensive. Starters include onion soup, leeks vinaigrette, and almost-forgotten dandelion greens with bacon

Chez Paul

and poached egg. Main courses of steak tartare, grilled beef, rabbit, veal, and farm raised chicken have been offered for years. After a dessert like baba au rhum, you'll be ready to face the rest of the day—or maybe take a nap!

Chez Paul Interior

Cartouche Café

12ᵗʰ ARRONDISSEMENT

We happened on the Cartouche Café at No 4 rue de Bercy when we were exploring the old quarter where wine was imported and stored before Bercy became part of Paris. We loved it! A chalkboard spans the wall with lots of choices. Starters included asparagus au gratin, lamb terrine with figs, and sautéed calamari. The scallops with saffron sauce were divine, as was the beef with sauce béarnaise. *Riz au lait*, the French version of rice pudding, was served with a peach confiture. There is no décor as such, just happy eaters.

The Place de la Nation straddles the border with the 11th Arrondissement. In its center is the obligatory statue of Marianne, the symbol of the French Republic. The two columns at one end marked a gate in the Farmers-General wall where taxes were once collected on goods entering the city. The Place de la Nation is a circle with both large and small streets radiating from it like spokes on a wheel. One street, the rue Jaucourt, is only a block long but appears to end in a village of its own with a town square look. The small bistro, Carpe Diem, at number 4, fits right in. My brother and I heard about this unassuming place and tried it on a wintry day. The first thing we noticed were the two chic young women who were running the place, one behind the bar and one working the tables, engaging in multiple running conversations with the regulars, who seem both hip and still old fashioned. One of the plats de jour on the chalkboard was the ideal lunch for a day like this, *hachis Parmentier,* beef hash under pureed potatoes,

Staff at Carpe Diem

baked in its own casserole, a little like a shepherd's pie. Dishes that use potatoes like this are named after Antoine Parmentier, the first agronomist to promote the potato as food for people instead of just for animal feed. The hachis was served with a salad. A glass of Bordeaux was the perfect companion. We will definitely return for several reasons, two of them being the charming staff.

13th ARRONDISSEMENT

The 13th Arrondissement is undergoing a lot of change. New university buildings and student housing are popping up along the Seine among pockets of old Asian food stores and restaurants. The working class ethic still prevails along the rue de Tolbiac where the No 62 bus bisects the 13th from east to west. The side streets have a 1950-1960 forgotten look, and that is where good traditional food is still served. Le Barrault-Vins, at 70 rue Barrault, is what the Parisians would call *un bijou* (a jewel). The red awning over the small terrace used the words *cave* and *bistro*. The restaurant's name is a play on words. It is pronounced the same as

Le Barrault-Vins

Bar aux Vins. Get it? Wine is sold from the racks inside. Ordering a bottle with a meal costs 5 Euros over the retail price. A chalkboard was propped against a table; 12 Euros for two courses. I'll translate. Starters: lentil salad, melon with ham, fresh vegetable plate, country pâté, herring and potatoes in oil. Main courses: pan fried wild boar sausage, veal stew in cream sauce, beef with tagliatelle noodles, skate fish poached with steamed potatoes.

They had me at the lentil salad—and the 12 Euros. The French do wonders with green lentils. These were cooked but still firm and served cold in a vinaigrette with onions, carrots, and smoked ham. I looked around. A lot of the others had also ordered

Le Barrault-Vins, salad de lentilles

them. I sipped a glass of Bordeaux. The *blanquette de veau* arrived. The sauce was not too heavy—just right. Behind the bar, Daniel, the owner sporting a graying pony tail, directed the action under the exposed beams of the dining room. Looking around, I saw young people in jeans, men in suits, and grandmothers in dresses. I joined them in using some of my crusty baguette to wipe the rest of the sauce from my plate. I should have worn a beret! I asked about the dessert I saw everyone ordering. It was clafoutis, an apple tart covered with a baked custard. It was delicious.

A bistro that combines cooking from France's southwest with the Basque country could be dangerous. Chez Gladines at number 30 on

Chez Gladines

the rue Cinq Diamants has the look of a workers' refueling stop. The neighborhood is becoming hip, and a younger crowd now takes up a lot of the tables at lunchtime. I spied a young man finishing a plate of something with a beige cream sauce. I asked the waitress what it was. "*Escalope de veau* à la Montagnard, *monsieur, c'est très bon."* I ordered it without the benefit of seeing what size it was to start with. It was unbelievably good, but the size was more appropriate for a *Montagnard*, a *very* big mountain man. I had the server write down the ingredients as I was devouring it. Thinly scalloped veal, smoked country ham, potato slices sautéed to a crisp in duck fat, sliced mushrooms, melted Cantal cheese, all covered in tarragon cream sauce and finished on the plate in the oven. They had my favorite wine from the Southwest of France, Madiran, by the carafe. It held up nicely to the rich sauce. I don't know how I managed it, but I had to try the Basque cake, an almond filled flan. I walked the long way home as pennance, but thinking of Edith Piaf, and humming *"Non, je ne regrette rien."*

14th ARRONDISSEMENT

The grand cafés on the boulevard Montparnasse are good, but do not qualify as neighborhood restaurants. They are more for long, slow meals, maybe Sunday lunch, and they are on the pricey side. As usual, the side streets hold the key to genuine local food.

The Crêperie Josselin at No 67 rue du Montparnasse (not the boulevard) is one of eleven on this short street known as "little Brittany."

They all serve Breton crêpes, but Josselin is our favorite. The Breton lace lampshades light up the wood paneled dining room, evoking a country inn. Long tables are full of diners enjoying brown, buckwheat flour crêpes filled with every conceiv-

Crêperie Josselin

able combination of meat, fish, cheese, vegetables, and eggs. They are washed down with pitchers of sparkling cider served in earthenware bowls. Sweet dessert crêpes usually follow for most everyone. This is one of the cheapest and most fun lunch places in the city.

I almost didn't include the bistro Les Petits Plats at 39 rue des Plants as a favorite. I was being selfish, trying to keep it all for myself. But I relented. If you go to only one place in this section for a weekday lunch, let it be this one. A fairly nondescript façade houses a 1910 era

bistro, featuring wood and brass fixtures with a genuine worn patina— even a cracked mirror behind the bar. Their motto is "Cuisine ca- naille", meaning for the common people. But there is nothing com-

Les Petits Plats

mon about the food. It is beautiful! It makes everyone in the place smile! Don't look for beef Burgundy or coq au vin. They create sensa- tional dishes that defy categories. When I sat down, a plate of toasted baguette slices and a ramekin of homemade tapenade quickly arrived as an *amuse bouche*, or appetizer, a nice touch. I'm embarrassed to say that I ate all of it. The menu du jour had one starter and one main course. My French wasn't good enough to understand what they were, but I saw the young, hip-looking wait staff bring what looked like the

Les Petits Plats

same dishes to everyone. I said, "*Je prends le menu du jour*", the best decision I ever made. I took a photo of the chalkboard and looked them up later. The first course was *velouté du Barry*, a creamy, thick cauliflower soup. On

top of it were sprinkled bits of nut and chorizo, just enough for the nuance. I loved it! What followed was another surprise, a *ballotine de volailles,* chicken breasts pureed with herbs, eggs, double cream, and tarragon, then made into sausages without skins. It was served over ri- sotto in a bisque. But there was something else! Black seeds gave it a wonderful smoky taste. I asked and was told they were roasted butternut squash seeds. I continued to be amazed with the dessert. An entire peeled and poached pear with a tiny scoop of caramel ice cream and crumbled brown sugar. They understand that a hint of something is more seductive that a dollop! All this at neighborhood prices.

15ᵗʰ ARRONDISSEMENT

The largest arrondissement in Paris, the 15th, is heavily residential and has a working class pedigree, a sure guarantee of having great

neighborhood restaurants. One of them, the Café du Commerce, is near our apartment. In 1921, it opened as a bouillon, serving beef and broth to workers from the nearby automobile factories, and later began expanding the inexpensive menu. The recently updated dining room has a retractable skylight ceiling. Waitstaff climb the stairs between the three levels with full trays amid the noise made by hungry locals. Leeks vinaigrette, eggplant with goat cheese, roast chicken and steak frites

Café du Commerce

highlight the lunch entries. We go there when we are shopping in this pleasant neighborhood. The address is 51 rue du Commerce.

The Café Chastel, at 77 rue Lecourbe, makes first timers feel like regulars. It is a genuine Auvergne restaurant, adored by nearby workers and older couples taking lunch as their main meal. Vintage rugby posters hint at the big appetites of their followers. The menu is simple.

Café Chastel

Starters like poached egg with mushrooms and country pâté, four different mixed salads, duck, veal and beef, all in their sauces, follow traditional family recipes. Tarte Tatin, an upside down apple tart, is one of the special desserts.

16ᵗʰ ARRONDISSEMENT

Just because the 16th follows the 15th numerically doesn't mean they have anything in common. Across the river from the working class neighborhoods is the land of the "*gratin*"—the upper crust of Paris. It contains the former villages of Passy and Auteuil, now both enclaves of the wealthy. But there are still good neighborhood "throwbacks" to anoth-

Le Beaujolais d'Auteuil

er era that are revered by the locals. Near the old Gare d'Auteuil is a delightful village café, Le Beaujolais d'Auteuil, on the corner of the boulevard Montmorency and the rue Poussin. Dinner size portions at lunchtime include smoked salmon salads, *Fricassé* of veal kidneys, duck breast, and farm raised chicken. The wine list includes several crus of Beaujolais. We ended our Auteuil walk with a late lunch there.

La Favorite

In Passy, La Favorite, surrounded by boutiques at 39 rue de Passy, is our favorite for the best warm goat cheese salad in Paris. The café is bright and full of ambience. Lunches are mostly lighter fare. Just what is needed for a break from shopping in this village of fashion boutiques.

17ᵗʰ ARRONDISSEMENT

Le Petit Villiers, 77 avenue de Villiers, is also known as "Chez Fred" after its owner. It caters to local office staff who like reasonably priced traditional midday meals. A lively crowd starts flowing in around one o'clock and doesn't stop for the next two hours. There

Le Petit Villiers

may be a short wait, but Fred will find a table for you. Rabbit terrines, steak tartare, and grilled salmon are hurried through the dining room and set at tables of hungry diners. There is no wasted effort among the staff at this busy place.

Another restaurant starting with "petit" is Le Petit Salé at 99 avenue des Ternes. This classic one room dining spot attracts a combination of young couples and suits from nearby offices, creating a soothing level of conversation. The walls are lined with vintage posters. My wife tried the avocado gratinée with Roquefort cheese, an unlikely combination. It was delicious and the waiter told us how to make it at home. I start-

ed with the country pâté served with *cornichons* (pickles) from Lemans. For main courses she had the cassoulet and and I had the chicken breast with a light mushroom sauce, both autumn classics. We wanted a me-

Le Petit Salé

dium carafe of red wine. The owner told us they didn't have carafes but he would bring an entire bottle and charge us for what we drank. This could have been dangerous, but we paced ourselves and only drank half.

18th ARRONDISSEMENT

If Montmartre is your destination, avoid the tourist traps on the Place du Tertre and try the Moulin de la Galette on the other side of the summit at 83 rue Lépic. It sits under an old windmill, one of two still standing on the hill. Dances once took place here. They were memorialized in Renoir's *Bal du Moulin de la Galette*. It's usually filled with locals at lunchtime when specially priced menus are offered from noon to two o'clock.

The back side of Montmartre is like the dark side of the moon to most tourists. They never see it. A few blocks down the hill from the Moulin de la Galette, at 65 rue Caulaincourt, is Le Cépage Montmartrois, a classic bistro that takes up the entire corner of an angled building. When we want oysters, this is our go-to place. They are widely known—but not to tourists—for having a large, fresh selection of shellfish from Normandy and Brittany. After sharing a "tasting platter" containing four different kinds of oysters and a half bottle of chilled Chablis, we chose the seven-hour lamb for two, always tender. We sipped a Rhône valley red. We watched as others were served the "royal seafood platter" consisting of oysters, pink shrimp, langoustines, mussels, crab, and lobsters. We envied them their appetites. The ochre-hued dining rooms in this century old neighborhood gem gave us a warm feeling on a cold day.

19th ARRONDISSEMENT

The 19th Arrondissement is not for Paris beginners. The film, *La Vie en Rose*, is full of scenes of the rough neighborhood where Edith Piaf grew up. The main attraction here is the parc des Buttes Chaumont; it's located on a hill that was once a quarry for limestone and gypsum. It opened in 1867 as one of the exhibits for the Universal Exposition. Most Paris parks are flat. This one has cliffs, waterfalls, and faux temples. Near the Buttes Chaumont Métro stop and the entrance to the park is a quiet neighborhood with two great little restaurants.

On the corner of the rue du Plateau is Le Bar Fleuri. If the Smithsonian museum had an exhibit of a typical Parisian neighborhood

Le Moulin de la Galette

Le Cépage Montmartrois

bistro, this place would be in it. Old varnished walls, red checkered table cloths, chalkboards with the plats du jour, and for some reason, an antique gas pump near the door. The patronne behind the

Bar Fleuri

Bar Fleuri Interior

bar does not see it as a fragile movie set. It is a humble place where the denizens of this quarter stop for coffee, lunch, or dinner. I had the *poulet fermier rôti* (roasted farm raised chicken) and *frites*, with some slightly chilled Beaujolais. You can't make a bad choice here.

A few blocks away at 9 rue du Tunnel is L'Endroit, a hip-looking restaurant with its own terrace, on the roof of the one story dining room. The daily menu contained starters of *crème de lentilles* (my favorite), rabbit terrine, and poached eggs with foie gras. Main courses were steak with béarnaise sauce, quiche Florentine, and roasted veal (my choice). I had the baba au rhum, with plenty of rhum, for dessert. There

A l'Endroit

are big crowds of young people here during warm weather because the dining room and the terrace are filled for lunch and dinner.

20th ARRONDISSEMENT

The 20th Arrondissement is on the move and becoming hip, meaning new options exist for dining out. La Boulangerie is set in a former bakery. In its own words, it "… has the allure of an old Parisian bistro … flirting between tradition and modernity." This has been the hot, new place since 2005, even though it's not new anymore.

One cold day in early January we started with the *rillettes de saumon*, coarsely chopped smoked salmon wih dill and crème, followed by their own take on *hachis Parmentier*. Despite its popularity, prices at lunch have

La Boulangerie

remained reasonable. The address is 15 rue des Panoyaux.

There is also the old balancing the new at Le Bistro du Parisien. There is no pretense about who they are. They serve locals and Parisians from across the city. I doubt if they have ever seen tourists. We've had lunch there several times when we were walking the Charonne neighborhood. The bistro is authentic without trying to be. I looked

Le Bistro du Parisien

up some customer reviews, all in French. The word used repeatedly to describe Le Bistro du Parisien was that it is "*correct*", which in French means, "This place is for real!" Grilled lamb with lentils, terrines with figs, duck breast in wine sauce, roasted and pureed potatoes. There are hundreds of other hidden places like this in Paris, and we aim to find more of them. The address, 31 rue Pelleport, is on a quiet street. Try it, but don't tell everyone!

It should be obvious by now that when it comes to food and dining out, we place a high value on quality, tradition, and authenticity. We never rush to try a newly opened restaurant with a celebrity chef, or the one that *Tout Paris* has just discovered or was just featured in the *New York Times*. We'll probably get around to them if they have staying power, but we prefer to find our own gems where we can take friends. The new discoveries, especially the small, family owned ones, become friends themselves.

Epilogue

riends in the US ask us, "What do you do for six weeks in Paris?" We answer that we lead a fairly low-key life. We walk a lot, use public transportation, and shop daily for food. Every evening and weekend afternoon there are concerts in venues around the city, many of them free. The suburban trains take us to historic villages, cathedrals, and châteaus. We also like to try new places for lunch. Basically, we are different people when we are there. The City of Paris goes to great length to entertain its citizenry. There are festivals in every month of the year. Carousels and ferris wheels spin during holidays. The Romans believed the best way to avoid citizen revolt was to "give them bread and circuses." This could easily apply to Paris.

It's been ten years since we bought our apartment. Strange things began happening as we passed that anniversary. A woman who lives in our building, with whom we had never exchanged anything but bonjours, came up to us at our favorite restaurant to discuss our choices for dinner. We were invited to the *"fête des voisins"*, a meet-your-neighbor night held across the street in front of the school where everyone brings a dish to pass and the wine flows freely. They all seemed to know us as "les Américains", and were anxious to learn about our home state, *La Caroline du Sud*. We began hearing, "Let's have a drink sometime." Some now address us with the familiar *tu* instead of *vous*. The manager of the wine store on rue Cler asked if

View of Eiffel Tower

we wanted them to save some of our favorite wine before it sold out. The *équipe* (team) at Le Florimond sent us a Happy New Year card. At La Terrasse we are now shown to "our" table in the corner by the

Paris Night

window. The French are polite to be sure, but there is a zone of famil-
iarity that is reserved for people they know well. We had discovered
how long it takes to enter that zone, in our case ten years! Had we lived
there year round instead of only seasonally, it probably wouldn't have
taken as long. After encountering us for a decade, they must have accepted that we were part of the neighborhood.

But our Parisian quarter is changing! Retired couples older than
we are have begun to sell their apartments at prices they could never
afford to pay today and are moving to residences for seniors. Younger professional couples, whose double incomes enable them to buy at
the high prices, are moving in. Nannies walk their children to school,
a sight never seen in the neighborhood when we first arrived. The old
post office building is being converted into expensive condos. Our
favorite newsstand just closed, the owner retiring. A luxury boutique
selling smoked salmon and caviar is opening in its place. We realize
that this is the opposite of a neighborhood in decline, and friends tell
us we should be happy with the upward trend, but we have become
emotionally invested in the Parisian lifestyle we have known. Still, the

changes have not altered some of the basic routines of a middle class quarter: bake sales by the Boy and Girl Scouts after church on Sunday, firemen selling calendars door to door, young girls offering bunches of *muguets* (lilies of the valley) on May Day on the rue Cler. Paris is one of those cities in the world where people like to say, "You should have been here ten years ago." We don't think we will ever live in Paris year round. The spring and fall seasons are a delight, but at the end of our visits we are always happy to exchange the blue, white, and red for the red, white, and blue and return home.

Our time in this city has taught me that Hemingway was right. There is never any ending to Paris. That means no one can know everything about it. There is so much more to discover that *Paris 201* could easily be followed by *Paris 301*. I am just the latest one of the millions to have been seduced by the city of light and its people, and one of the thousands who have tried to put it into words.

Jerry Martin

Acknowledgments

My thanks to the special people who assisted me with this book: To my son Brian whose idea of buying an apartment in Paris gave us the courage to take the plunge, and for his photographs that complement the text. To Chuck Bradley who taught me how to write 50 years ago and who for the past four years patiently edited each chapter, using his red pen and sharp wit to reteach me some of the basics. To Carol Bradley for her encouragement. To my son Aaron who helped find a wonderful publisher. To Sandrine Wathey for elevating the level of my French spelling and grammar and for providing insights that only a native Parisienne would know.

Dôme at Dusk

Index

Boulevard Charonne métro

C

Eiffel Tower

Montmartre Windmills

rue St-Dominique